T0194809

# CHRISTIANITY AND **QUANTUM PHYSICS**

Analogies between Christian Teachings
and Quantum Physics Laws

**Samuel Padilla Rosa, PhD**

WESTBOW
PRESS®
A DIVISION OF THOMAS NELSON
& ZONDERVAN

WestBow Press books may be ordered through booksellers or by contacting:

WestBow Press
A Division of Thomas Nelson & Zondervan
1663 Liberty Drive
Bloomington, IN 47403
www.westbowpress.com
844-714-3454

ISBN: 978-1-6642-5949-2 (sc)
ISBN: 978-1-6642-5950-8 (hc)
ISBN: 978-1-6642-5948-5 (e)

Library of Congress Control Number: 2022903881

Print information available on the last page.

WestBow Press rev. date: 07/22/2022

"It is by faith we understand that the whole world was made by God's command so what we see was made by something that cannot be seen."

—Hebrews 11:3

"Quantum Physic makes visible the invisible and marvelous works of God's Creation."

—Samuel Padilla Rosa, PhD

# INTRODUCTION

This work proposes an approach to Christian religion teachings and the laws that govern modern scientific principles, especially Quantum Physics. It also aims to show the surprising analogy: the relationship of similarity or comparison between the Christian religion and scientific teachings in light of new interdisciplinary scientific discoveries in postmodern science. Science and religion are the two most critical significant worldviews. They are considered as two opposing worldviews which that cannot coexist side by side. However, this work is about how both disciplines, the Christian religion and science, have implications in the psychic life and spirit of the twenty-first-century Christian. It attempts to attest to the spiritual processes of the believer because of the new findings of Quantum Physics. Its main purpose is to bring hope and encouragement to the Christian, who not only is part of the biological world as the rest of the living beings of creation but is also the owner, from his very nature, of a neurophysiological support that leads him the transcendence from the material realm to the spiritual realm and from that platform to be a useful instrument at the service of Christians in these times, when science is multiplying by leaps and bounds.

When we observe the scientific and technological advances that take place daily, such as the discoveries of subatomic particles of matter in laboratories, we are amazed at the wonderful work of God's creation. This book's main objective is to present the striking analogies between Christian teachings and Quantum Physics Laws, the latter of which makes the invisible works of God, visible.

Quantum Physics says that light behaves in waves.[1]

"God is light" —"God is Spirit" — (John 4:24)

His Spirit is analogous to the natural light's wave nature of natural light. (It cannot be seen nor touched).

The True Light that gives light to everyone came into the world. The Word became flesh and made his dwelling among us. They saw his glory as One who came from the Father (John 1:14).

The Word—Jesus Christ; the True Light, incarnate—came in the flesh to the world. This is analogous to the light's corpuscular nature (in that photon can be seen). This work aims to link, imply, and relate science to religion—, specifically, the Christian faith.

There are many biblical references, both in the Old Testament and in the New Testament, that point to Jesus, the founder of Christian teachings, as light. That Word (the abstract Word, whose behavior is in waves—God) became flesh (matter, corpuscle, particle, visible body)—Jesus, the Word. Before he died on the cross, according to the Christian teachings, he was with his disciples as matter, with a visible body (corpuscle). Before coming to the world and after his resurrection, He was transformed in Spirit, analogous to light's wave nature (invisible, abstract).

This work aims to link, imply, and relate science to religion—specifically the Christian faith. It intends to apply the research results and knowledge of the various science disciplines to the theological understandings to strengthen the principles that govern and sustain the Christian faith. It intends to establish the relationship between biological processes and spiritual processes that give humans their unique position among all of creation's species.

---

[1] https://www.ducksters.com/science/physics/light_as_a_wave.

# CHAPTER 1
## Newton, Descartes, and Darwin

Until now, biology and physics have been the masters of the views of Newton, the father of modern physics. The things we believe in—our world and our place in it—are rooted in ideas formulated in the seventeenth century, which remain the backbone of modern science. These theories present all the universe's elements as being isolated from each other, which creates a world of things separated from each other. Newton described a natural world in which the individual particles of matter follow specific laws of motion through time and space.

While Newton presented his laws of motion to the whole world, the French philosopher René Descartes proposed a revolutionary notion and said that we, represented by our minds, were separated by this inert matter from our bodies. This notion was another thing—a kind of magnificent oiled machine. The world, Descartes said, was made up of small, discrete objects that behaved predictably. The most separated of these objects was the human being. We were outside the universe as mere spectators; even our bodies were somewhat isolated from the real nature that we were—the conscious mind as an observer.

The Newtonian world may have been law-abiding, but it was ultimately a deserted and desolate world. With some skillful movements, Newton and Descartes were able to uproot God and the spirituality of the world of matter and our consciousness from the center of our authentic being. Newton and Descartes uprooted our minds and souls from the spiritual realm and left a trail of a collection of beings evolving through the survival of the fittest and through random multiplication.

With the works of Charles Darwin's theory of evolution, the desolation in the human, created in the image and likeness of his or her Creator, was made even sadder. "Be the strongest, or you will not survive." "You are just an evolving accident." "Eat, or the strongest will eat you." "The essence of your humanity is a genetic terrorist who does not respect gender or species, effectively undoing the weakest links." "Life is about consistently winning, being the first to arrive, and if you manage to survive, you're on your own alone at the top of the tree of evolution." "They all went astray; together, they became useless; there is no one who does good, there is not even one."[2]

## The Involution of Humankind

In her blog post titled "Emotional Involution of the Human Being," Verónica Gutiérrez Portillo says the following about the involution of the human being: "Incredible and difficult to understand that in the second decade of the XXI century and contrast to the immense advances in science and technology, the human being takes gigantic steps backward in her nature. As science and technology continually evolve and advance, human beings walk emotionally in parallel in involution."

[2] Romans 3:10–12(NIV)

That paradigm—the world as a great machine, and humankind as a surviving machine—has led the world to be powered by technology, but with little or no knowledge of who we are and our relationship with the Creator and the universe. From the spiritual point of view, this has led us to return to a worse degree than the animals to which humankind was entrusted to exercise dominion over them, give them a name and take care of them

All of Newton's and Descartes's knowledge did not lead us to an understanding of the fundamental mysteries of our being: how life began, how a single cell develops until one becomes a fully formed person, how we think, or, even further, what our relationship is with the Creator of the entire universe.

We became ardent apostles of these visions of a mechanized and separate world, even though this was not part of our everyday experience. Many of us seek to quench the thirst for transcendence to even higher levels of spiritual consciousness in existing religions from the paradigm of biology. This quest can give us a certain sense of security for their ideals of unity, community, and purpose, but from one point only—from a purely biological point of view proposed by science alone. Anyone seeking to quench their spiritual thirst has to deal with these two opposing visions and paradigms—science on the one hand and spirituality on the other—and try unsuccessfully to reconcile the one with the other.

A little over a hundred years ago, Albert Einstein finished a scientific article that would change the world. His radical vision of the nature of light would help transform Einstein from an unknown patent clerk to the genius at the center of twentieth-century physics.

All physicists in 1905 knew what light was, either from the sun or any other sources. The light was known as a wave—a succession of equally separated ridges and depressions where the distance between the peaks or the lows determines the color. All scientists knew without a doubt that light originated from a source, was distributed evenly, continued through all accessible space, and spread from one place to another as electromagnetic ridges and depressions. The light was called an electromagnetic wave, or, more generally, electromagnetic radiation. In 1905, the wave nature of light was an established and indisputable fact.

Here is a parallel between God's Spirit and the wave of natural light. The natural wave of light is intangible, abstract, and cannot be seen; God's Spirit is also intangible, abstract, and cannot be seen. Like the wave of light that cannot be seen, God cannot be seen either. "No one has ever seen God, but if we love one another, God lives in us, and his love is made complete in us. God is spirit, and his worshippers must worship in the Spirit and truth" (John 4:24).

Given this universally held knowledge, scientists proposed that light was not a continuous wave but consisted of localized particles. They argued that when a ray of light spreads from one point to another, the energy is not continuously distributed over ever-larger spaces but consists of a finite number of quanta of energy. These limited quanta are located at points in space, and they move without dividing and can be absorbed or generated only as a whole.

In the last fifty years, with the discoveries of quantum physics, technological achievement has come at such a dizzying pace that it has advanced the world in ways once only imagined in science fiction. Some of these innovations transformed our daily lives, such as electricity, the radio, the TV, fiber optics, computers, and the internet. All these inventions, and many others, have become necessities in our everyday lives.

We saw airplanes leave their propellers on the ground and, with their powerful jet engines, soar through the air at high speeds until they broke the sound barrier. On July 20, 1969, an estimated 650 million people watched in suspense as Neil Armstrong descended a ladder toward the surface of the moon. They not only saw him walking on the moon but also heard him saying at the same time, "That's one small step for man. One giant leap for humankind."

We are living in a special time. Never have such intense, radical technological changes taken place. Something extraordinary was discovered about reality along the way.

According to the Spanish newspaper *El Mundo*, the European Organization for Nuclear Research (CERN) has just written a crucial chapter in the history of physics by discovering a new subatomic particle that confirms with more than a 99 percent probability the existence of the Higgs boson, popularly known as the "God particle"—a fundamental finding to explain why matter exists as we know it.[3] What they found was the particle that gives mass to all the particles in the universe, the Higgs boson particle—"the particle of God."[4]

---

[3] Miguel G. Corral, "They discover the 'God particle' that explains how matter is formed," El Mundo, 2012, https://www.elmundo.es/elmundo/2012/07/04/ciencia/1341398149.html.

[4] According to an article in the *Guardian*, to mark the eightieth birthday of the man behind the elusive particle (God particle), a competition to rename it was held. The particle became known as the Higgs boson in 1972 after Ben Lee, a former head of theoretical physics at Fermilab, used the name to describe the idea. But the origins of the name go back to Fermilab. In the early 1990s, the former director of the lab, Leo Lederman, wrote a book on particle physics that he called *The God Particle*; Ian Sample, "Anything but 'The God Particle,'" the *Guardian*, Friday May 29, 2009, https://www.theguardian.com › may.

# CHAPTER 2

## Christianity

---

## The Foundations of Christianity

Christianity (from the Latin "christianismus," which is from the Greek "χριστιανισμός") is a monotheistic Abrahamic religion based on the life and teachings of Jesus of Nazareth. It is the largest religion in the world, with approximately 2.4 billion followers.

Christianity is a diverse religion both culturally and doctrinally. Its main branches are Catholicism, Protestantism, and Orthodoxy. Its adherents, called Christians, share the belief that Jesus is the Son of God and the Messiah (in Greek, "Christ") prophesied in the Old Testament. He suffered, was crucified, descended into hell, and rose from the dead for the salvation of humanity.

Christianity emerged from Judaism in the middle of the first century AD in the Roman province of Judea. The first leaders of the Christian communities were the apostles and their successors, the apostolic fathers. This early Christianity spread, despite being a minority and persecuted religion, through

Judea, Syria, Europe, Anatolia, Mesopotamia, Transcaucasia, Egypt, and Ethiopia. Christianity was legalized in the Roman Empire by the Edict of Milan in 313. Emperor Constantine converted to Christianity and convened the Council of Nicaea in 325, in which the Nicene Creed was formulated. Christianity became the Roman Empire's official religion in 380, under Emperor Theodosius I the Great. Since then, Christianity has been, in its different branches, the dominant religion on the European continent. During these first centuries, the church fathers gradually consolidated the doctrines of Christianity and elaborated the canon of the New Testament.

## The Communion of the Eastern Churches

The church of the first seven ecumenical councils is often referred to as the "Great Church" because the Catholic Church, the Orthodox Church, and the Eastern Orthodox Churches were in full communion. The Eastern Churches separated after the Council of Chalcedon (451) as a result of Christological differences. The Catholic Church and the Orthodox Church separated in (1054) because of disagreements about the authority of the pope of Rome. Protestantism, a collection of denominations, first appeared during the Protestant Reformation of the sixteenth century. Protestants criticized what they perceived as significant theological and ecclesiological deviations on the part of the Catholic Church. The discovery of America in (1492) spread Christianity throughout America. The Catholic Church promoted the Counter-Reformation in response to the Protestant Reformation through the Council of Trent (1545–1563). Judaism shares some of its holy writings with Christianity. Together with the Greek Bible, the Tanach, older than the Tanach in its present form, constitutes the basis for the Old Testament of the various Christian Bibles. For this reason, Christianity is considered an Abrahamic religion, along with Judaism and Islam.

## Different Opinions about the Date of Jesus' Death

Some twentieth-century studies do not take AD 33 as an incontrovertible date for the death of Jesus Christ. Some suggest that there could be a lag of four to eight years between the beginning of the calculation of the Christian era and the precise date of the birth of Jesus of Nazareth, known as Christ. In addition to this, there is no apparent certainty or consensus among these authors that he died at the age of thirty-three.

Christianity came to be considered a sectarian doctrine of the Orthodox Jewish traditions in its early decades. Since Christianity became the Roman Empire's official religion in the fourth century, it has significantly influenced Western culture and many others.

The word "Christianity" comes from the Greek word "χριστιανός" ("christianós" ["Christian"]), which in turn comes from the proper name "Χριστός" ("Christós" ["Christ"]), a translation of the Hebrew word "Messiah," which means "anointed." The term's origin appears in the book of Acts of the Apostles, where the disciples are called Christians for the first time. "… and when he found him, he brought him to Antioch. So for a whole year, Barnabas and Saul met with the church and taught great numbers of people. The disciples were called Christians first at Antioch." (Acts 11:26 NIV).

## Historical Development of Christianity

Christianity has its historical origin in the Second Temple Judaism of the beginning of the present era. Although Jesus of Nazareth always identified himself as a devout Jew, in his doctrine and teachings, he said,

"I am the way and the truth and the life. No one comes to the Father except through me". (John 14:6 - NIV)

"Again, Jesus spoke to them, saying," I am the light of the world. Whoever follows me will not walk in darkness but will have the light of life". (John 8:12 - NIV)

## Christianity in the Twentieth Century

Christianity in the twentieth century was characterized by accelerated fragmentation. The century saw the rise of liberal and conservative groups and a general secularization of Western society. The Catholic Church instituted many reforms to modernize itself. The missionaries made inroads into the Far East, establishing followers in China, Taiwan, and Japan. At the same time, persecution in communist Eastern Europe and the Soviet Union brought many Orthodox Christians to Western Europe and the United States, increasing contact between Western and Eastern Christianity. Furthermore, ecumenism grew in importance, beginning at the Edinburgh Missionary Conference in 1910, although it is criticized that Latin America has been excluded because Protestant preaching in Latin America has frequently been anti-Catholic.

Another movement that grew in the twentieth century was Christian anarchism, which rejects the Christian Church, state, or any other power except that of God. Christian anarchists believe in absolute nonviolence. The book by Leo Tolstoy called *The Kingdom of God Is within You*, published in 1894, was the catalyst for this movement.

In the 1950s, there was an evangelical expansion in America. The post-WWII prosperity experienced in the United States also had religious effects, termed "morphological fundamentalism." The number of Christian temples increased, and the activities of the evangelical churches grew expansively.

Within Catholicism, liberation theology (LT) formally emerged in the 1960s in Latin America as a response to the malaise produced by the oppression and poverty characteristic of the peoples of this region. The Catholic Church does not officially accept the postulates of LT, owing to a possible close relationship with Marxism, although liberation theologians deny such a relationship. But they do accept the existence of concepts such as the class struggle. However, the Catholic Church does accept some postulates of the same LT, especially in relation to the need for freedom of the peoples in the world, but also generalizing the idea to freedom from other sins as well.

## The Rise of Pentecostalism

Another notable twentieth-century development within Christianity was the rise of Pentecostal movements. Although its roots date back to before 1900, its actual birth is commonly attributed to the twentieth century. Sprouted from Methodist roots, it rose from meetings at an urban mission on Azusa Street in Los Angeles. From there it spread throughout the world, carried by those who experienced what they believed to be God's miraculous movements there. Pentecostalism, which started the charismatic movement within established denominations, continues to be a major force in Western Christianity.

### Modernism and the fundamentalist reaction

The radical implications of scientific and cultural influences by the Enlightenment were noted in the Protestant churches, especially in the nineteenth century; liberal Christianity sought to unite the churches together with the broad revolution that modernism represented. In doing so, new critical approaches to the Bible were developed, new attitudes became apparent about the role of religion in society, and new thinking began to question the almost universally accepted definitions of orthodox Christianity.

In reaction to these events, the Christian fundamentalism movement rejected the radical influences of philosophical humanism because they affected Christianity. Targeting especially the critical reaches of the interpretation of the Bible and trying to block the inroads made into their Christian churches by atheistic scientific assumptions, the fundamentalists began to appear in various denominations as numerous independent movements of resistance to the abrupt changes of historic Christianity. Over time, the evangelical fundamentalist movements had split into two branches, one labeled fundamentalist and a more moderate movement that preferred the evangelical label. Although both movements originated first in the Anglo-Saxon world, evangelicals are now found everywhere.

## The Rise of the Evangelical Movement

There has been significant growth in the evangelical sector of Protestant denominations in the United States and the rest of the world, especially those that identify themselves exclusively as evangelical, and a decline in those churches identified with more liberal currents. In the interval period (the 1920s), liberal Christianity was the fastest-growing sector, which changed after the Second World War, when more conservative leaders arrived in the ecclesiastical structures.

The evangelical movement is not an entity. Evangelical churches and their followers cannot be easily classified. Most are not fundamentalists, in the strict sense that some give that term, although many continue to refer to themselves as such.

However, the movement has managed to develop informally, to reserve the name "evangelical" for those groups and believers who adhere to a profession of Christian faith that they consider historical—a paleo-orthodoxy, as some call it. Those who call themselves "moderate evangelicals" claim to hold even closer to these "historical" Christian foundations, and "liberal evangelicals" do not apply this appellation to themselves in terms of their theology but rather in terms of their "progressive" lives in the civic, social, or scientific perspective.

# CHAPTER 3

## Quantum Physics

At the beginning of the twentieth century, scientists assumed that they had discovered all the fundamental laws and rules that govern our existence. It was not until physicists began studying particles of matter using new technologies that they discovered an entire sublayer of physics involving tiny and mysterious units of matter and energy. This discovery left them bewildered and unable to fully explain the phenomena that, with innovative instruments, appeared before their eyes. Thus was born this strange and mysterious truth—quantum physics. The universe can be understood only as a network of interconnection. How can electrons be in contact with all things at once?

When the pioneers of quantum physics peered into the very center of matter, they were amazed at their findings. The smallest particles of matter were not even matter as we know it—not even a stable thing. Stranger still, many possibilities were shown at the same time. It was also strange that these subatomic particles do not have an isolated meaning but concern everything else. Matter cannot be cut into its most minor units in its most elemental state, but it is entirely indivisible. The universe can be understood only as a network of interconnection. How can electrons be in contact with all things at once? How can an electron not be a stable thing until it is captured, measured, and examined by the observer? Things, once in contact, will always stay in touch through time and space. The observer interacts with the observed. Space-time appears as arbitrary constructions that are no longer applicable to this level of Newton and Descartes' world, let alone Darwin's. In this new vision, all we see is a vast quantum plain of the here and now, made up of tiny light-charged particles that hold the entire universe together. Physicists believed that a tiny particle of matter, if ever found, could explain the mysterious code at the origin of the physical world. To know this would be "to know the mind of God," as some scientists said.

In the past fifty years, innovation has come at such a dizzying pace that it has transformed our world in ways once imagined only in science fiction. These are some of the most influential developments over these fifty years: automatic teller machines, DNA testing and sequencing, electric cars, fiber optics, noninvasive laser and robotic surgery (laparoscopy), photovoltaic solar energy, bar codes and scanners.

## The CERN Experiment

As recently as July 4, 2012, scientists from the Large Hadron Collider announced the discovery of the Higgs boson, known as "God's particle."[5] Scientists from the "ATLAS and CMS experiments at CERN's Large Hadron Collider" announced that

---

[5] The Large Hadron Collider, the world's largest and most energetic particle accelerator, uses a twenty-seven-kilometer-circumference tunnel created for the Large Electron and Positron Collider (LEP), and more than two thousand physicists from thirty-four countries and hundreds of universities and laboratories participated in its construction..

in each of these experiments they had observed a new particle in "the mass closest to the 126 GeV region." According to scientists, this particle is consistent with the Higgs boson, predicated on the Peter Higgs model.

In the (CERN) experiment, at speed equal to that of light (300,000 k/s), positively charged protons collided head-on. What scientists were looking for with this was what they already had theorized the existence of—the massive Higgs boson, named for Peter Higgs, who searched for the origin and ultimate constituents of matter. His goal was fundamental physics.

## Scientists Find "God's Particle"

The massive Higgs boson, crucial to the search for the origin and ultimate constituents of matter, was recently confirmed by ATLAS and CMS experiments at CERN's Large Hadron Collider through the discovery of the predicted fundamental particle. This particle is what gives mass to the other particles. In this way, the matter is composed; and therefore, the origin of all things in the universe is justified.

"From microscopic algae to the largest planet in the galaxy, which passes through humans, everything is made up of elemental particle matter bound together by a type of glue that makes up the Universe and everything known."[6] Some scientists say that this glue is analogous to the Spirit of God, which permeates the entire universe, and that everything is united by it. In a way analogous to the Son as the image of the invisible God, through whom and in whom all things were created, all things hold together (Colossians 1:16).

The Higgs field, proposed in 1964 by the British physicist of the same name, forms the basis of the standard model of physics.

---

[6] David Horsey, "Higgs Boson Binds the Universe, but Humans Give It Meaning," *Los Angeles Times*, July 5, 2012, https://www.latimes.com/politics/la-xpm-2012-jul-05-la-na-tt-higgs-boson-20120704-story.html.

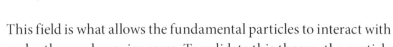

This field is what allows the fundamental particles to interact with each other and acquire mass. To validate this theory, the particle associated with the Higgs field, the Higgs boson, had to appear, and that is what they found.

## (CERN) Experiment—An Analogy for God's Creation

Beyond the stars, in the confines of the galaxies, beyond the quasar 3C273, located about 3,000 million light years away, in Virgo, a tremendous explosion was heard and felt. It was the Creator of the universe, sailing through the sky at a speed of 300,000 k/s, the speed of light, making his angels spirits and the flames of fire his servants. (Hebrews 1:7). That massive beam was God, because God is light (1 John 1:5).

# CHAPTER 4

## The Dual (Wave–Particle) Nature of the Natural Light Analogous to God's True Light Dual (Spirit–Matter) Nature

At the beginning of the twenty century all physicists knew what light was, either from the sun or any other source. All scientists knew without a doubt that light originated from a source, was distributed evenly, continued through all accessible space, and spread from one place to another as electromagnetic ridges and depressions. The light was called an electromagnetic wave, or, more generally, electromagnetic radiation. The wave nature of light was an established and indisputable fact.

**Genesis: God's Creation**

In the beginning, the earth was formless and empty, darkness was over the surface of the deep, and the Spirit of God was hovering over the waters (Genesis 1:2). It was such a large and imposing depth that its bottom could not be found. The lack of light produced absolute darkness, and therefore the deep was devoid of life. There is no life without light. There is no life without Jesus, the light of this world (John 1:4).

A roar echoed as the Creator and the whole army of the heavens burst into the history of the beginning of our world. The earth was shaken. The foundations of the mountains shook. He lighted coals. He descended from the heavens, and there was thick darkness under his feet. He rode on a cherub and flew on the wings of the wind. He put darkness near his hiding place by wrapping his curtain around himself: dark waters and clouds from the heavens. Near the brightness of his presence, his clouds emitted hail and burning coals. The Lord thundered in the heavens, and the Most High gave his voice, hail, and fiery coals. He sent his arrows. Then the abysses of the waters appeared, and the foundations of the world were exposed. (Psalm 18:7-5). "And God said, 'Let there be light,' and there was light. God saw that the light was good, and he separated the light from the darkness. God called the light 'day,' and the darkness he called 'night.' And there was evening, and there was morning—the first day" (Genesis 1:3–5).

Throughout the rest of the book of Genesis, God continues to create the world's splendor: the sky, the earth, the ocean, the sun, the moon, the creatures, and, finally, humankind. The light was the first thing God created. According to quantum physics, the light was essential to create the other things, since his design requires the force of light to unite the different particles of matter.

## God's Light, Analogous to the Natural Light

God, the "True Light of the World" (John 1:9), has all the characteristics of the natural light. Here is an analogy of the natural light with God as light. Just as scientists say that light has a dual (wave–particle) nature, God has a dual (spirit–matter) nature too.

"God is Spirit" (John 4:24). Just as you cannot see the wave nature of light, you cannot see God's Spirit either (John 1:18). But as the wave's disturbance moves energy from one place to another, the Spirit of God moves from one place to another, hovering over the waters (Genesis 1:1, 2).

The substance that a wave moves through is called the medium. That medium moves back and forth repeatedly, returning to its original position. But the wave travels along with the medium. It does not stay in one place. Just as the wave travels along with the medium, the Spirit of the Lord in Jesus went through all the towns and villages, teachings in their synagogues, proclaiming the good news, and healing every disease (Matthew 9:35).

Analogous to the wave's medium is Jesus Christ, who acts as the mediator (medium) between God the Father and humankind. There is one God (the True Light) and one mediator (medium), Jesus, between God and humankind—the man Christ Jesus. (1 Timothy 2:5).

Infrared light, also known as infrared radiation, is one type of light outside the visible range. You cannot see this light, but you can feel its heat, though it is unlikely you will be burned by it. Like infrared radiation, the Spirit of God is everywhere; you can hear his sound, as happened in the garden, but cannot tell where it comes from or where it is going. This is so with everyone born of the Spirit. (John 3:8). The Spirit of God is like infrared rays; you cannot see his light, but you could be burned, as the prophet Jeremiah was when he was not to mention the word of God anymore, but the word of God was in his heart like a fire; he was weary of holding it in, but he could not (Jeremiah 20:9).

Jesus, the incarnation of God (Spirit), can be seen; this is analogous with a particle of light (a photon), which can be seen.

Light is radiation that propagates in the form of electromagnetic waves. Electromagnetic waves can propagate through a vacuum. Light is, therefore, electromagnetic radiation.

This phenomenon (the movement of energy) can occur in space or in matter (air, water, earth, and the like.).

The propagation of God's light could occur only through Jesus and in Jesus (matter). Likewise, when Jesus came out of the waters of baptism, he was filled with the Holy Spirit, and the same Spirit led him into the wilderness, where he fasted for forty days and forty nights and was tempted by the devil. Jesus overcame temptation, and with the Holy Spirit within him, he came to Galilee in the Holy Spirit and taught in their synagogues, and everyone praised him. From Galilee, Jesus went in the Spirit to Nazareth, where he had grown up, and on the Sabbath day, he went to the synagogue. They handed him the scroll of the prophet Isaiah, and when he unrolled the scroll, he found the chapter where it is written, "The Spirit of the Lord is on me because he has anointed me to proclaim good news to the poor" (Luke 4:1–18).

In the past, God spoke to our ancestors through the prophets many times and in various ways (Hebrews 1:2). But in these last days, as in the synagogue, God is speaking to us through the Holy Spirit, the advocate, whom the Father sent in Jesus's name on Pentecost. He is teaching us all things, and he is reminding us of all that Jesus said and that remains recorded in the scriptures to this day (John 14:26).

We have other lights that we cannot see but that we can feel. The Son, Jesus Christ, is analogous to the visible light spectrum.

God is light; in him, there is no dark (1 John 1:5). God so loved the world that he gave his one and only Son, that whoever believes in him shall not perish but shall have eternal life (John 3:16). The true light that gives light to everyone came into the world (John 1:9).

Visible light waves (waves in the visible light spectrum) are the only electromagnetic waves that we can see out of the entire spectrum of white light. We see these waves as rainbow colors, and each color is a wave that has a different wavelength.

Ezekiel saw the glory of God in the likeness of a rainbow. "Like the appearance of a rainbow in the clouds on a rainy day, so was the radiance around him. This was the appearance of the likeness of the glory of the LORD" (Ezekiel 1:28). Visible light is the portion of the electromagnetic spectrum that is visible to the human eye. Electromagnetic radiation in this wavelength range is called "visible light," or simply "light." A typical human eye will respond to wavelengths of approximately 390 to 700 nm. In terms of frequency, this corresponds to a band in the vicinity of 430 to 770 THz.

However, the spectrum does not contain all the colors that the human eye and brain can distinguish. Unsaturated colors, such as pink or purple color variations, are absent, for example, because they can be made only by mixing multiple wavelengths. Colors that contain only one wavelength are also called "pure colors" or "spectral colors."

Visible wavelengths pass through the optical window—the region of the electromagnetic spectrum that allows waves to pass unattended through Earth's atmosphere. An example of this phenomenon is clean air scattering blue light more than red wavelengths, making the midday sky blue.

# CHAPTER 5

## DNA—God's Intelligent Design

---

### The Creation of the Living Things of the Waters

"But they deliberately forget that long ago by God's word the heavens came into being, and the earth was formed out of the water and by water" (2 Peter 3:5). Peter's theological theory of the creation of every living thing out of the waters is in accord with that of the Greek philosopher Thales of Miletus and his cosmology based on water as the essence of all matter.[7]

On the fifth day of creation, as he had done during the entire creation process, God created the great creatures of the sea and every living thing with which the water teems and moves about, according to their kinds, and every winged bird according to its kind. And God saw that it was good (Genesis 1:21).

In the creation of living things and the great creatures of the sea, the mind of Christ, the Word creating at the beginning with

---

[7] Thales de Miletus or the First Greek Philosopher - https://humanfactor.blog/2020/04/27/ -

God (John 1:1–3), made a great design—a tiny molecule we call DNA.[8] In that tiny molecule, he encoded all the information for the different characteristics of those living things coming out from the waters.[9] In its due time, that small molecule had to begin reading the language that the Creator encoded in its genome, with the key to producing proteins that would encourage the development of living things, including the wondrous creatures of the waters, according to their gender.[10]

---

[8] Deoxyribonucleic acid, or DNA, is a molecule that contains the instructions an organism needs to develop, live, and reproduce. These instructions are found inside every cell and are passed down from parents to their children. DNA is made up of molecules called nucleotides. Each nucleotide contains a phosphate group, a sugar group, and a nitrogen base. The four types of nitrogen bases are adenine (A), thymine (T), guanine (G), and cytosine (C). The order of these bases is what determines DNA's instructions, or genetic code. Human DNA has around 3 billion bases, and more than 99 percent of those bases are the same in all people. www.livescience.com.

[9] Bacteria are microscopic single-celled organisms that exist in their millions in every environment, both inside and outside other organisms. Some bacteria are harmful, but most serve a useful purpose. They support many forms of life, both plant and animal, and they are used in industrial and medicinal processes. Bacteria are thought to have been the first organisms to appear on earth, about 4 billion years ago. https://www.medicalnewstoday.com/articles/157973#:~:text=Bacteria.

[10] A genome is an organism's complete set of DNA, including all of its genes. Each genome contains all of the information needed to build and maintain that organism. In humans, a copy of the entire genome—more than 3 billion DNA base pairs—is contained in all cells that have a nucleus. Microscopic organisms are tiny life forms, often consisting of a single cell, and very sensitive to change. They are vitally important in the food chain and to the health of our planet. They are the base of the marine food web and, directly or indirectly, are food for everything else in the open sea. In addition, these microscopic organisms have a role in maintaining the Earth's atmosphere – they help remove carbon dioxide and release chemicals that help form clouds. Scientists study microscopic organisms in the Antarctic so they can better understand atmospheric changes and the depletion of the ozone layer. http://www.antarctica.gov.au/

## The Creation of Adam in the Image of his Creator (Genesis 1)

On the fifth day of creation, the Creator, as he had had done during the process of creating the living things and creatures of the water, said, "'Let the land produce living creatures according to their kinds: the livestock, the creatures that move along the ground, and the wild animals, each according to its kind.' And it was so. God made the wild animals according to their kinds, the livestock according to their kinds, and all the creatures that move along the ground, according to their kinds. And God saw that it was good …" (Genesis 1:23–24).

On the sixth day of creation, God returned, as he had previously done, to pronounce the Creative Word and said, "Let the earth bring forth living creatures according to their kind, beasts and serpents and animals of the earth after their kind" (Genesis 1:24–25).

Then, in the mind of the Word, in the genome of that same tiny structure, DNA, with which he had created the things and the creatures of the waters, God codified its language and reading in the earth's animals to be developed according to their genders, the livestock according to their genders, and all animals that crawl on the earth according to their species and to their DNA genome codes.[11] The Creator did not leave them to chance, as the theory of evolution says, but in the DNA of each living being, there is a genetic code from the mind of the Creator, which directs its development. The Creator used the same DNA molecule structure as the basis for creating the things and creatures of the waters and the beasts of the earth. "So, God created mankind in his image

---

[11] "A *genome* is the complete set of genetic information in an organism. It provides all of the information the organism requires to function. In living organisms, the **genome** is stored in long molecules of DNA called chromosomes. Small sections of DNA, called genes, code for the RNA and protein molecules… https://www.nature.com/scitable/definition/genome-43

in the image of God he created them; male and female he created them" (Genesis 1:27).

In Genesis (1:26), God was creating in the mind of the Word (Christ) the image of humankind. It was on the sixth day that Elohim said, "Let us make man in our image" (Genesis 1:26). On this occasion of humankind's creation, God did not say, as he had said during the creation of Darwin's biological animals, "Let the earth produce living creatures" (Genesis 1:24). Now God said, "Let us make man in our image …"

"The Human Genome"[12] Study and "Understanding Evolution", from Berkely University[13], both studies agree with the order of creation in the story of the book of Genesis. First came the creatures of the waters, the birds that fly in the sky, and the animals of the earth, and then humankind was created in the Creator's image and likeness. All of them, including humankind, have the DNA structure as the base for their creation. The difference is that in humankind's DNA genome, God encoded new information, a new language, a new genomic code—namely, the code of the image of the Creator.

"So God created mankind in his own image, in the image of God he created them, male and female he created them" (Genesis 1:27).

Adam's DNA contained the information and coding to procreate and fill the earth, subjugate it, and lord it over the fish of the sea, the birds of the heavens, and all the beasts that move over the earth. His DNA also contained information of what he must eat for his subsistence, and, above all, the ability to communicate with his Creator.

God also inscribed in humankind's DNA the kind of food humankind could eat. He did this not only in humankind's DNA but in animals' DNA too (Genesis 1:29–30).

---

[12] www.ncbi.nlm.nih.gov › pmc › articles
[13] https://evolution.berkeley.edu/examples-of-homology/legs-and-limbs/

This same information of what they should eat or not eat would appear inscribed in Darwin's animals' DNA. But In addition to Adam's DNA having basic information for subsistence, feeding, and procreation like that of the rest of the animals, Adam's DNA had the additional information for coding an additional "neurophysiologic support" to store information that implied his having been created to the image of his Creator (His Creator Spirit "in" him, His image inside of him). This distinguished him from all other created beings through the human brain, with its 100 billion neurons and 1.2 billion glial cells. This neurophysiologic support, the brain in Adam, contained the science, the wisdom, the intelligence, and the mental capacity to maintain a close relationship with his Creator and master all things created, including the universe.

## The Creation of Adam in Likeness of his Creator (Genesis 2)

This is the account of the heavens and the earth when they were created when the LORD God made the earth and the heavens. Now no shrub had yet appeared on the earth, and no plant had yet sprung up, for the LORD God had not sent rain on the earth, and there was no one to work the ground, but streams came up from the earth and watered the whole surface of the ground. Then the LORD God formed a man from the dust of the ground and breathed into his nostrils the breath of life, and the man became a living being. (Genesis 2: 4–7)

Genesis 2 is not a mere repetition of creation but is the physical manifestation of all that God created in the mind of Christ—of things that could not be seen in chapter 1. "So we fix our eyes not on what is seen, but on what is unseen since what is seen is temporary, but what is unseen is eternal" (2 Corinthians 3:18).

Humankind, created in the mind of the Word (Christ), is created (spiritual) in Christ's image in Genesis 1. Now, in chapter 2, humankind, who was formed in his likeness, becomes visible in the sensitive reality.

Everything we can see is made up of things we cannot see—particles that are called "quanta." Quantum mechanics describes the behavior of matter in all its details and the happenings on an atomic scale. Things on a microscopic scale behave like nothing that you have any direct experience of whatsoever. They do not behave like waves, do not behave like particles, do not behave like clouds or billiard balls or weights on springs or anything that you have ever seen.

The scriptures say, "By faith, we understand that the universe was formed at God's command so that what is seen was not made out of what was visible" (Hebrews 11:3). We could say that at the end of the seventh day, everything had been created in the mind of Christ, the Word. "The Son is the image of the invisible God, the firstborn over all creation. For in Him all things were created: things in heaven and on earth, visible and invisible, whether thrones or powers or rulers or authorities; all things have been created through him and for him. He is before all things, and in him, all things hold together" (Colossians 1:15–17).

## The Power of Words in Creation

According to recent scientific studies, the vibration of words excites or inhibits DNA.[14] Thus, every time the Word, Christ (the

---

[14] Researcher Dan Winter, who developed a computer program to study the sinusoidal waves emitted by the heart under emotional responses, in a phase of research with his colleagues Fred Wolf and Carlos Suárez, analyzed the vibrations of the Hebrew language with a spectrogram. What they discovered was that the pictograms that represent the symbols of the Hebrew alphabet corresponded exactly to the figure that makes up the wavelength of the sound of each word. That is, the shape of each letter was the exact figure that formed that wavelength when

Light of the World) pronounced the Word, the waves of light (photons charged with electromagnetism) shot at a speed of 300,000 km per second, ready to excite the molecules of matter and promote the design thought by the Word, Christ, in chapter 1 of Genesis. On that occasion, in chapter 1, the Creator, the Word, created in his mind the image of himself in Adam.

Everything that exists was first a thought. That is perhaps why there is repetition in the text quoted above. Man was first created in the mind of the Creator (invisible) in Genesis 1"... before it was visible on earth ..." in Genesis 2. —The Creator already had designed in his mind Adam, the man, down to the color of his hair, of his eyes, of his skin; his stature; and other characteristics encoded in his DNA.

This process of God's creation is analogous to the building of a house. First, the concept comes about in the mind, according to the needs and tastes of the owner. Then the plan is developed, with its aesthetic and scientific specifications. (See Genesis 1.) After the design of the project is approved and ready, it is made visible with sand, stone, water, cement, blocks, finishes, furniture, and so forth. (in Genesis 2.)

## The Likeness of Adam to his Creator

"Then the LORD God formed a man from the dust of the ground and breathed into his nostrils the breath of life, and the man became a living being" (Genesis 2:7). Whereas in Genesis 1 God the Creator gave his "image," his Spirit, to Adam (the

---

being vocalized. They also verified that the symbols that make up the alphabet are geometric representations. In the case of the Hebrew alphabet, the twenty-two glyphs used as letters are twenty-two proper names originally used to designate various states or structures of a single sacred cosmic energy, which is the essence and semblance of all that is.Masaru Emoto was a Japanese author known for his controversial claims that words, sentences, sounds, and thoughts directed towards a volume of water would influence the shape of ice crystals obtained from the water.

Spirit being analogous to a light wave in that it is abstract and cannot be seen), here in Genesis 2 the Creator forms him in the Creator's likeness and makes him visible (analogous to the light's particles).[15] "... rather, he made himself nothing by taking the very nature of a servant, being made in human likeness" (Philippians 2:7).

All human beings on this planet are direct descendants of that man, Adam, created in the image of his Creator (God) and formed in his likeness from the dust of the earth (Son) and with the breath in his nose (Holy Spirit), the breath of life of his Creator. As such, we carry the same code of Adam's DNA. In that code is inscribed the image and likeness of the Creator. Adam was a special being created as a living soul, but he had the Spirit of God in him to maintain a special relationship with his Creator. Unlike Darwin's animals, God had equipped Adam with neurophysiological support (the brain), making Adam capable of communicating with his Creator.[16] The couple could see him (their Creator) and even talk with him in the garden, which was possible because the Spirit of God, his image, was in Adam. His Spirit was the specific element that allowed this. Such communication was possible because when God created Adam, he imparted on Adam intellect and spirit, which had rewarding consequences. But it turned out that God had placed a condition on the garden's inhabitants to continue enjoying that communion and the benefits of living in

---

[15] "Likeness" means "The semblance, guise, or outward appearance of..." https://www.merriam-webster.com/dictionary/likeness.

[16] The central nervous system (CNS) controls most functions of the body and mind. It consists of two parts: the brain and the spinal cord. The brain is the center of our thoughts, the interpreter of our external environment, and the origin of control over body movement. Like a central computer, it interprets information from our eyes (sight), ears (sound), nose (smell), tongue (taste), and skin (touch), as well as from internal organs such as the stomach. The spinal cord is the highway for communication between the body and the brain. When the spinal cord is injured, the exchange of information between the brain and other parts of the body is disrupted. www.christopherreeve.org.

Eden. They should not break the supreme law and should not eat from the Tree of Knowledge of Good and Evil, for they would die if they did (Genesis 2:15). "For what the law was powerless to do because it was weakened by the flesh, God did by sending his own Son in the likeness of sinful flesh to be a sin offering. And so, he condemned sin in the flesh the likeness of the flesh of sin and because of sin, condemned sin in the flesh" (Romans 8:3).

## The Garden of Eden

"Now the LORD God had planted a garden in the east, in Eden, and there he put the man he had formed" (Genesis 2:8). This story is fundamental because it explains the true nature of our life here on Earth. It tells us about ourselves, our state of being, and how we produce the conditions we live in. It is the model experience of all of us here on Earth and of our destiny. When people fully understand this story of the garden of Eden, they will understand our Creator nature and evil nature. This parable is placed at the beginning of our human history because it is the foundation on which the whole creation plan is built. From Genesis to the Apocalypse, all Bible's revelation assumes an understanding of the garden of Eden's great principles and characteristics, in which the Creator put the first couple he had created.

We could call this story a parable because Jesus spoke all these things to the crowd in parables. He did not say anything to them without using parables. So was fulfilled what was spoken through the Prophet: "I will open my mouth in parables, I will utter things hidden since the creation of the world" (Matthew 13:34–35).

So if a parable is just a story, why not call it a story? Why use an unusual word like "parable" if a common comment like "story" can do it? The answer is simple: this word is used because a parable is more than a story. It's a story plus it has a bonus added to the story. It has two things that run side by side: the lesson and the reality.

In their ignorance of the garden of Eden's meaning, many people seem to think that Eve symbolizes women as sex and that in some way Adam represents men as sex as well. The truth goes far beyond this; Adam and Eve in the garden represent all humanity in the first Adam, the human being who lives, who has lived, and who will live on Earth. What happened to us happens in the rest of the humans as well. What they were, so are all humans. Our experience is the experience of the whole of humanity. Our destiny is the destiny of the entire human race. What was happening to them in the garden speaks of realities even today. It is the whole humanity who are represented in the garden, not only the couple, but all humanity who are confronted, loved, directed, accused, expelled, instructed, and redeemed.

The book of Genesis is, then, the beginning, the innocence, the guilt, the redemption, and the perfection of every man and woman. What happened there is what is happening to humanity in the here and now. The couple in the garden represent: *what* man and woman are, and *why* man and woman are. They represent man and woman as we know them, with all their capacities and potentials, under the influence of their Creator. They were created as purely spiritual beings in the image and likeness of their Creator, but by disobedience to the Higher Law, they fell into the merely biological realm, like the rest of the animals that God created.

## The Tree of Knowledge of Good and Evil

"But of the tree of the knowledge of good and evil you will not eat, because the day you eat from it, you will certainly die" (Genesis 2:17). In the Jewish and Christian tradition, the Tree of the Knowledge of Good and Evil, and the eating of its fruits, represents, in the book of Genesis, the beginning of the mixture of good and evil at the same time. Only biological beings, such as vegetation and lower animals, were subject to the cycle of death and life. The human, created in the image and likeness of his Creator, was not subject to evil, death, corruption, and other evils that afflicted other living beings. There was no free choice before eating the forbidden fruit; there was evil as an entity separate from the human psyche, and it was not in human nature to wish for it. Eating and internalizing the forbidden fruit changed all this, and thus the evil inclination was born.

According to the biblical story in Genesis 1, there is no death on the Tree of Life: "The Lord God said: Behold, the man is like one of us, knowing good and evil; Now, therefore, let him not reach out his hand, and also take of the tree of life, and eat, and live forever" (Genesis 3:22).

The good is the joy of seeing the vegetation of abundant green leaves, multicolored and beautiful flowers, abundant fruits for food, and the species' survival in summer. But it is sad, too, in winter to see the arid and desolate fields, and dry, leafless trees and plants. Biological beings are subjected to the tragic cycle of life and death. It is the human drama of good and evil: pain and pleasure, death and life, joy and sadness, love and hate.

In Freud's psychoanalysis, we find that in the unconscious, the life instincts, or Eros, are characterized by the disposition they create in the subject to form ever greater units. Eros is always an appetite for union, and, for example, it manifests itself in love, sexual activity, and the desire to maintain one's physical and psychic unity. On the other side is Thanatos, the death instinct. Because of the death instinct, we find in the subject an appetite for the state of total tranquility, the cessation of stimulation and activity, an eagerness to return to the initial inorganic state. This instinct is fundamental to other positive instincts, forming together with the life instinct, or Eros, fundamental dispositions of every living being, including humans. Masochism, sadism, and all desire for destruction is a pathological expression of the instinct of Thanatos—death.

## The Forbidden Fruit

There are several theories regarding the kind of fruit the couple ate in the garden of Eden. One of them is the mistranslation of the Latin word "*malum-mal*" (evil) for the term "*malus*" (apple). Other theories say that the forbidden fruit was the fig, since the leaves used to cover their nakedness were those of the fig tree—a beautiful tree.

Cider, an apple product, is an intoxicating drink. The word "cider" comes from the Latin "*sicĕra*," which in turn comes from the Hebrew "šēkāt" (intoxicating drink, product of the apple). Hence there seems to be a tradition of pointing to the apple as the forbidden fruit.

Whatever the forbidden fruit, the truth is that eating said fruit—and even more so, disobeying the Creator's law—caused the separation of humankind from the Creator. After they ate the forbidden fruit, both Adam and Eve afraid hid among the trees of the garden because they heard the Lord's footsteps walking in the air of the day. For the first time, the couple's psyches were seized by the emotion of fear.

Diet includes foods and beverages as well as alcohol and drugs, which alter the states of consciousness of those who consume them and which, with prolonged use, can alter or modify the DNA's reading. The consumption of alcoholic beverages causes a memory deficit in the hippocampus. In women, the toxic effect is more pronounced than in men, because they metabolize it different. The alcohol releases dopamine, giving rise to a pleasant stimulus. Some molecules, such as amphetamines, cause intellectual doping, increasing dopamine in memory networks and holding memories for a short time. To speak, imagine, reflect, reason, calculate, decide, or plan the future, we need memory that is managed in real time and keeps the stored information present.

We do not keep in our memories everything that happens around us; however, if the intensity of a stimulus is strong, that experience is fixed and stored in long-term memory. The more sensitive or emotional we are regarding an incident, the more details we memorize, causing an increased sense of reality. The lived and the known configure the autobiographical memory.

The desire to transcend is the primary appetite of the soul. The need to transcend seized the psalmist so strongly that he came to envy the sparrow and the swallow for being near the Lord's altar. "Even the sparrow has found a home, and the swallow a nest for herself, where she may have her young—a place near your altar LORD Almighty, my King and my God (Psalm 84:3).

When, for whatever reason, men and women fail to transcend themselves through worship, good deeds, and spiritual exercises, they are inclined to resort to the chemical substitutes for religion—drugs. If we look around, we can see how legal and illegal drugs, including alcohol, are being consumed in ever-increasing numbers.

## The Tree of Life

The Tree of Life is a widespread motif in many myths and folk tales worldwide, by which cultures tried to understand the human and profane condition concerning the realm of the divine and sacred. Many legends speak of a Tree of Life that grows on the ground and gives life to gods or human beings, or a world tree, often linked to the center of the earth. It is probably the oldest human myth and perhaps a universal myth.

In ancient Egyptian mythology, the gods had their seat in a sycamore, *Ficus sycomorus*, the fruits of which were intended to feed the blessed. According to the Egyptian Book of the Dead, twin sycamores flanked the eastern gate of heaven, from which the sun god, Re, emerged each morning. This tree was also considered a manifestation of the goddesses Nut, Isis, and especially Hathor, the "Lady of the Sycamore." *Ficus sycomorus* was often planted near graves, and it was believed that a dead man buried in a coffin of this wood returned to the womb of the mother tree goddess.

The Tree of Life was often taken as the center of the world. It was seen as a union of heaven and Earth, representing a vital link between the worlds of the gods and humans. Oracles, judgments, and other prophetic activities took place in its shadow.

The Tree of Life of the kabbalah (medieval esoteric doctrine of Jewish mysticism) had ten branches, the *Sefirot*, which represented the ten attributes or emanations by which the infinite and the divine would enter relation with the finite.

The branched chandelier called the menorah, one of the oldest symbols of Judaism, is related to the Tree of Life. God would have dictated the shape of the menorah to Moses; it was to have six arms with cups in the form of almond blossoms, with buds and flowers. In the book of Proverbs, he also tells us that wisdom is "a tree of life for those who take hold of it" (Proverbs 3:18).

The so-called world tree, or cosmic tree, is another symbol like the Tree of Life. There was a world tree in the garden of Eden of the book of Genesis, and this tradition is common to Judaism, Christianity, and Islam. There are Haitian, Finnish, Lithuanian, Hungarian, Indian, Chinese, Japanese, Siberian, and North Asian myths of the cosmic tree. Ancient peoples, particularly Hindus and Scandinavians, imagined the world as a divine tree born from a single seed sown in space.

The ancient Greeks, Persians, Chaldeans, and Japanese had legends that described an axis tree on which the earth rotated. Medieval kabbalists represented creation as a tree with its roots in the reality of the spirit (the firmament) and its branches on the earth (material reality). The image of the inverted tree is also seen in inverted postures in yoga, in which the feet are conceived as receptacles for sunlight and other heavenly energies to be transformed as the tree transforms light into other energies.

However, the most common belief is that the cosmic tree has its roots in the lower world and its branches in the highest reaches of the firmament. It has always been considered natural and supernatural at the same time—that is, belonging to the earth but somehow not of the earth itself. Encountering this tree, or living in or on it, usually means the regeneration or rebirth of an individual. In many epic tales, Eastern cultures conceive of the Tree of Life as sinking its roots into the sky and nourishing its trunk, branches, leaves, and fruits from heaven. The hero dies on the tree and is regenerated. There is also the idea that the world tree told the story of the ancestors, and to recognize the tree was to recognize the place of the individual as a human being.

The neuroanatomical term "arborvitae" (tree of life) describes the branching pattern between the cortical gray matter and the subcortical white matter of the cerebellum.

Many beliefs of different philosophies and religions see the Tree of Life as being inverted, sinking its roots into the sky. Judeo-Christian teaching teaches that the Creator, God, is the source of all creation, wisdom, knowledge, and intelligence. The book of Proverbs says that the Lord laid the earth's foundation and, by wisdom and by understanding, set the heavens in place (Proverbs 3:19). From the Lord comes the wisdom, and from his mouth comes knowledge and understanding. (Proverbs 2:6). Proverbs also teaches that "the Tree of Life is the fruit of the righteous" (Proverbs 11:30). According to the Book of Revelation, the eating of the Tree of Life is for the one who overcomes (Revelation 2:7).

According to the scriptures, we can affirm that wisdom, intelligence, knowledge, the fruit of the Spirit, all come from God, from the Father of Light. That Light, whose source comes from heaven, is analogous to a rainbow on a rainy day; its Light is reflected in the natural world as the fruit of the Spirit. "The fruit of the Spirit is love, joy, peace, patience, kindness, goodness, faith, meekness, and temperance; against such things there is no law." (Galatians 5:22–23).

As the sacred text says, every good gift and every perfect gift descends from on high from the Father of lights (James 1:17).

According to Christian Neuro Theology,[17] the spiritual activity of hearing, thinking, and meditating on the Word of the Creator, God, which comes from the higher spiritual regions, causes the activation of sensations and electrical discharges in the brain (from electrical and bioelectric synapses) that are subject to perception by the individual who experiences them. That is to say, the internal spiritual perceptions of the brain can be perceived, interpreted, and defined, and meaning obtained from them, like many other experiences where there are emotions, activation of memories, or learning activities.

No other sense can perceive such memories. These are issues between the hypothalamus, thalamus, and their complicated afferent pathways to the cortex. These are perceived as chemical signals coming from this brain region and reaching the cortex, which, by translating these signals, transforms them into electrical signals, which in turn are the perceptions that we call "directive function."[18]

So the arborvitae, for Christians, is analogous to the neurophysiological support of the central nervous system. The human brain is made up of billions of neurons and billions of astrocytes that reside in the brain. These billions of brain neurons are in synaptic communication day and night, through biochemical and electrochemical currents with each other. These communicate all the information perceived either by the natural senses or by the abstract perceptions of thoughts, with which we know, abstract, communicate, learn, remember, and communicate with the Creator. This directive function of the brain is the

---

[17] "Christian Neuro Theology" is one of the emergent disciplines of Neuroscience"
[18] Dr. Héctor Colón Santiago, President, founder, of "Christian Neuro Theology" University of Puerto Rico.

metaphor of the Tree of Life, whose roots sink into heaven, in the unfathomable immensity of the council of the Creator.

Eden's memories, as exquisite as dreams, weave their threads of light in all peoples' traditions. No nation under heaven does not give the beginning of our race as being from some distant period of purity, peace, and harmony with nature and with the whole universe. The hieroglyphics of Egypt, the clay tablets of Assyria, the Edda of Scandinavia, the legends of Tibet, and Rome's bas-relief tell the same story of primitive bliss. Everyone wants to prove the truth of the statement that the Creator (God) planted a garden eastward in Eden and put the man he had formed there. But the garden of Eden is not simply a piece of real estate somewhere in Mesopotamia. Such a place has not been found, nor has the angel with his flaming sword at its entrance, charged with keeping humans out. It is not surprising that humans have sought it, but they have sought it in vain because they seek it outside of themselves.

The garden is not a physical place located on this or any other planet. It is a *state of being*. It is a higher existence for a human than this involuted state in which we find ourselves in physical birth. It is the state of being in which humankind was taken out of the Creator's hands and placed here on Earth. It represents humankind in the presence of the Creator; a human with incorruptible life available, created in the image and likeness of the Creator, as master over all things; a human living on sickness, pain, and death. And yet the garden also represents humankind along with all the internal and external environmental factors and conditions that would ultimately lead to his ruin and estrangement from his Creator. In a certain sense, humankind was the garden—a garden inside a garden, a world inside the creation.

Adam and Eve could not stay after being tempted and ending up disobeying what God had asked them not to do. God had no alternative but to fulfill his promise and comply with the death sentence. But we observe that Adam and Eve's physical deaths did not occur immediately. Rather, they were expelled from the garden. But in that expulsion, something profoundly serious happened. The promise of God was fulfilled to perfection, and they died regarding the image of God that dwelled in them. The Spirit of God that dwelled in them died. The image of his Creator was withdrawn from them. God allowed them to maintain the intellect, but God's Spirit in them cannot live with sin, and therefore they died to that spiritual dimension. They had known they died to the possibility of continuing to live in the garden of Eden and to continue in constant communion with God. Adam and Eve continued their existence, alienated from communion with their Creator.

"When Adam had lived 130 years, he had a son in his own likeness, in his own image; and he named him Seth" (Genesis 5:3). God created Adam in his own image and his own likeness. But Adam begot Seth first in his likeness and then in his image. Here the order of creation is reversed. The image of God was no longer in Adam. The disobedience left Adam without the image of his creator in him. Now Adam created his own thoughts and his own ways, because just as the heavens are higher than the earth, so are God's ways higher than Adam's crooked ways (Isaiah 55:8–9).

Seth's older brothers, Cain and Abel, had already been born. Cain had killed Abel, the one who offered the right sacrifice before God. The marks of the disobedience in Cain's genes, transmitted by the genetic inheritance of his father, Adam, gave expression to his emotions of envy and hatred, ending in the killing of his brother Abel (Genesis 4:1–16). Only Cain remained, an exile wandering the earth.

Now, with the birth of Seth, begotten in his father Adam's "likeness according to his image,[19]" Adam's offspring follow him with the mark of sin in his DNA's genome. Because we bear the mark of sin in the image (spirit of disobedience) of Adam in us,

---

[19] Genesis 5:3

in this way death came to all people, because all sinned. (Romans 5:12).

We are born with the likeness and image of Adam, but without the image of the Creator. Adam passed on his own likeness and his own image to Seth, and Seth passed it on by genetic inheritance, or transgenerational heritage, to all of us to this date. Adam's likeness and image in us is a transference whereby the emotional, physical, and social pain suffered by Adam was transmitted by genetic inheritance to subsequent generations, in ways that go far beyond simply learned behavior.

Also, Adam and Eve were there, eating the forbidden fruit until "they heard the LORD God as he was walking in the garden in the cool of the day, and they hid from the LORD God among the trees of the garden" (Genesis 3:8). It was not until Adam and Eve heard God walking in the garden that they knew their actual existence away from their Creator. With this new state of consciousness, of confusion, of forgetfulness, of doubts, and of unlimited freedom, they had lost all contact with their Creator and had forgotten him. Suddenly they heard the footsteps of God in the orchard. At that moment, the couple began to feel different, separated from their Creator—from everything. It was a loneliness that separated them from each other, from their environment, and from God.

# CHAPTER 6

## Analogy Between Electromagnetic Radiation of Natural Light and the True Light of God

Quantum physics says everything is made of tiny subatomic bits, but what is the force that holds quantum particles, atoms, and molecules together? The answer is light. From microscopic algae to the largest planet in the galaxy, everything is made up of matter—elementary particles joined by a kind of glue that makes up the universe.

Light (from the Latin "*lux*") is electromagnetic radiation that, although not seen, can be perceived by the human eye through a prism. Jesus said, "I am the light of the world. Whoever follows me will never walk in darkness but will have the light of life" (John 8:12).

There are seven primary ranges of wave frequencies within the electromagnetic spectrum. While all these radiation types are photon streams, they differ in their frequency, wave amplitude, and energy content. These frequency ranges include radio waves, microwaves, infrared light, visible light, ultraviolet light, X-rays, and gamma rays.

The true light that gives light to everyone was coming into the world. The Word became flesh and made his dwelling among us (John 1:14). The prophet Ezekiel saw the glory of God, which is analogous to the electromagnetic spectrum. He saw the glory of God like the appearance of a rainbow in the clouds on a rainy day (Ezekiel 1:28).

The visible spectrum, or visible light, is the region of the electromagnetic spectrum that the human eye can perceive and translate into the various colors that we know.

The scriptures attest to the many visible manifestations of God to humankind (epiphanies). These have occurred through the elements of nature, especially fire, which produces light and purifies. God appeared to Moses and the people of Israel in fire. The angel of the Lord appeared to Moses in flames of fire (Exodus 3:2). God appeared to the couple in the garden in the air of the day (Genesis 3:8).

Of the entire spectrum of white light, the portion that humans can see, is tiny compared to the other spectral regions. The visible spectrum comprises wavelengths from 380 nm to 780 nm. In light's decomposition, the human eye perceives the light of each of these wavelengths as a different color. This electromagnetic radiation cannot be seen with the naked eye. No one has ever seen God, but the one and only Son, who is himself God and is in closest relationship with the Father, has made him known (John 1:18).

Electromagnetic radiation is a type of variable electromagnetic field, a combination of oscillating electric and magnetic fields that propagate through space, transporting energy from one place to another. This electromagnetic field that propagates through space, transporting energy, is analogous to the Spirit of God's presence throughout the universe "Where can I go from your Spirit? Where can I flee from your presence? If I go up to the heavens, you are there; if I make my bed in the depths, you are there. (Psalm 139:7,8).

## Radio Waves of the Electromagnetic Spectrum of Natural Light Analogy with of God's Light

Radio waves are used in a wide variety of applications: AM and FM radio, military communications, cell phones, amateur radio, wireless networks, and many more. Most radio frequencies can pass freely through the atmosphere, but some are reflected or absorbed by the ionosphere.

A mobile phone is a cellular radio transceiver, since it receives and sends radio signals. This is analogous to God's communication with humankind. Similarly, a radio transceiver, which receives and sends radio signals, is analogous to the Lord saying that if you call him, he will answer you (Jeremiah 33:3).

The DNA in the cell's nucleus has the compacted structural properties of a fractal antenna.[20] Analogous to radio communication, a transceiver, in a way is similar to DNA, can transmit and receive radio waves using an antenna for communication purposes. That is why the couple in the garden could heard the Lord's footsteps (Genesis 3:8).

## The Lord Manifests Himself to the Garden Couple in a Way Analogous to the "Radio Waves" of Natural Light's Electromagnetic Spectrum.

The man and his wife heard the Lord God as he was walking in the garden in the cool of the day, and they hid from the Lord God among the trees of the garden (Genesis 3:8).

---

[20] ResearchGate, "DNA Is a Fractal Antenna in Electromagnetic Fields," https://www.researchgate.net/publication/50986117_DNA_is_a_fractal_antenna_in_electromagnetic_fields.

A radio wave originates when an electron, located in the radio frequency zone, is stimulated.[21] This is analogous to people seeking the Lord do it *with* "their heart and with all their soul and with all their mind." (Matthew 22:37-40)

All electromagnetic waves travel through a vacuum or air at the speed of light. This is analogous to the Lord rising at one end of the heavens and making his circuit to the other; nothing is deprived of his warmth (Psalm 19:6)

Waves like radio waves generally constitute the part of the electromagnetic spectrum whose photon energy is too weak to break atoms. This photon energy weakness is analogous to the time when Jesus returned to his disciples and found them sleeping and reproached them for not having been able to watch (pray) with him even for an hour (Matthew 26:40).

## The Trauma of Adam's Fear

By listening to the Lord's footsteps in the garden, the couple's auditory sense was stimulated by the waves' sound. The couple's limbic system activated and automatically took control of the situation, producing immediate physiological changes without them having the opportunity to reason.[22]

The limbic system is made up of various brain structures that regulate physiological responses to certain stimuli. It comprises parts of the thalamus, hypothalamus, hippocampus, amygdala,

---

[21] Phillips, Melba and Fritzsche, Hellmut. "Electromagnetic radiation". *Encyclopedia Britannica*, 23 Jul. 2020, https://www.britannica.com/science/electromagnetic-radiation. Accessed 11 February 2022.

[22] The limbic system is a system made up of various brain structures that regulate physiological responses to certain stimuli. It is made up of parts of the thalamus, hypothalamus, hippocampus, amygdala, corpus callosum, septum, and midbrain. Adam could not reason because he had become disobedient, as Paul states: "For we too were once foolish, rebellious, lost, slaves of lusts and various delights, living in malice and envy, abhorrent, and hating each other" (Titus 3:3).

corpus callosum, septum, and midbrain. The amygdala, which provides our emotional defense, is the most essential structure within the limbic system. It is the one that saves and manages our most irrational emotions. This part of the brain, in which the "defense" is generated, produces the worst feelings of human beings: fear, anger, sadness, and emotional defensiveness. It is the most critical structure within the limbic system.

Adrenaline began to spill into the couple's bloodstreams, and just as in Darwin's animals, they no longer had the knowledge and science of their Creator to look for any answer.[23] They lost the ability to reason through their disobedience. They were left only with the animal instinct to stay and fight or to flee. They chose the latter—to hide, to flee from the presence of their Creator. The Spirit of their Creator, the image of him, was no longer in them, and the ability to reflect, reason, and anticipate the future, according to the Creator's plan for him, no longer existed. They hid, full of fear, among the garden trees.

Fear triggered countless physiological reactions that they no longer had control over. Cell metabolism increased along with blood pressure, their hearts began to beat rapidly, and their pulses quickened. They began to sweat, and their mouths became dry. They felt their breath escaping and had a feeling of suffocation and tightness in their chests. They felt nauseated, and they got dizzy. They thought that soon everything would get out of control and they would go crazy.

Theirs was a terrible fear of dying. They believed that, for disobeying and eating the forbidden fruit, death by an angry God would suddenly come upon them at any moment. Like the sword of Damocles, the phrase the Lord had spoken to them weighed

---

[23] Adrenaline is a hormone secreted by the adrenal glands that in stressful situations increases blood pressure, heart rate, and the amount of glucose in the blood, and accelerates metabolism.

on their heads: "… because the day you eat it, you will certainly die." (Genesis 2:17).

The night shadows, the noise of a restless animal, the howling of the wind, the movement of a tree branch—all these things, in their lonely minds, were ghosts that came to bring death to them. Now they expected they would suffer death at any moment for having transgressed the supreme order of their Creator. This threat caused them tremendous stress that did not allow them to be calm at night during sleep or in wakefulness during the day. They would undoubtedly die like any living being among Darwin's survivors.

"Among those nations, you will find no repose, no resting place for the sole of your foot. There the LORD will give you an anxious mind, eyes weary with longing, and a despairing heart. You will live in constant suspense, filled with dread both night and day, never sure of your life. In the morning, you will say, 'If only it were evening!' and in the evening, 'If only it were morning!'— because of the terror that will fill your hearts and the sights that your eyes will see" (Deuteronomy 28:65–67). The constant stress that all this entails contributes to an excess of cortisol, and its early breakdown in the blood produces the spread of free radicals, which have dire consequences for health.

Medical research has studied the effects of free radicals in the body in recent years. These are positive ions, atoms, or molecules that have lost an electron, so they become positively charged. I already stated that stress increases the number of free radicals in the body. These compounds play a crucial role in the genesis of cancer and cardiovascular diseases. As these free radicals are atoms or molecules that lack an electron in the body, they try to recover that electron, and they do so aggressively. When this process takes place inside cells, the cells lose a large part of their defensive capacity. Free radicals (or positive ions) damage the nuclei of cells, affecting the genetic material itself, so the cells degenerate, becoming carcinogenic.

By transgressing the supreme law of God, the couple lost the image of their Creator and lost the sense of spiritual perception. However, God allowed them to maintain the property that came with the bodily senses. They would have to find the good things in life and discard the bad by their own experimentation. That would bring them pain, suffering, and death—and not because of the science and wisdom that come from the light of God. For the Lord gives wisdom, and from his mouth come knowledge and understanding (Proverbs 2:6).

## The Pentecost Experience—Analogous to a Quantum Physics Leap

In quantum physics, a quantum leap is a sudden change in the physical state of a quantum system that occurs practically instantaneously. On the day of Pentecost, all the 120 gathered there were suddenly filled with the Holy Spirit and fire and began to speak in other tongues and received power (Acts 2:4). A sudden change (quantum leap) occurred to the disciples when they were full of fear, sadness and discourage, for the death of their Master, Jesus. Suddenly they are filled with the Holy Spirit and fire and began to speak in other tongues and received power.

## Radio Waves and the Quantum Leap

"The man and his wife heard the sound of the LORD God as he was walking in the garden in the cool of the day, and they hid from the LORD God among the trees of the garden" (Genesis 3:8). When the couple heard the footsteps of the Lord, they were afraid and hid among the trees of the orchard. The couple's fallen spiritual state prevented all contact with their Creator. The forbidden fruit numbed all their senses. At some point in that hour of tranquility and peace, when a fresh breeze was blowing in the garden, they heard the Lord's footsteps—not his voice, but only this noise, similar to the noise of static during the tuning of an AM radio. The couple tried to hide among the garden's trees, but now, without their Creator's science, knowledge, and wisdom, they did not know the effect trees can have on the radio wave reception. "Few people are aware of the effect trees can have on the reception of radio waves and microwaves. As with light, objects such as hills, buildings, or tall trees can obstruct or deflect these signals, creating deep shadow patterns in which reception is difficult. The screening effect of trees has a further disadvantage in that it can vary greatly with the season and weather conditions and is especially important in areas where the signals are weak."[24]

## The Quantum Leap to Microwaves

Microwave antennas are useful devices in radar, radio, satellite communications, and wireless communication systems. Different types of microwave antennas have different uses. Similarly, the DNA structure behaves as a fractal antenna, which can interact with electromagnetic fields over a wide range of frequencies.[25]

Since microwaves have higher energy than radio waves, they gave the couple the ability not only to hear the Lord's footsteps but also to see their nakedness (Genesis 3:10).

Microwaves are limited to line-of-sight propagation; they cannot pass around hills or mountains as lower-frequency radio

---

[24] BBC. "Help Receiving TV and Radio." https://www.bbc.co.uk/reception/questions/.
[25] M. Blank and R. Goodman. "DNA is a fractal antenna in electromagnetic fields." *Int J Radiat Biol.* 87, no. 4 (April 2011), 409–15. doi: 10.3109/09553002.2011.538130. Epub 2011 Feb 28. PMID: 21457072.

waves can. Similarly, John the Baptist said that in order to get the revelation of the glory of God, every valley shall be raised, every mountain and hill lowered; he said the rough ground would become level, and the rugged places a plain (Isaiah 40:4–6).

## The Quantum Leap to Infrared Rays

The main effect of the absorption of microwaves in materials is heating, in a way similar to infrared waves radiated by heat sources such as a space heaters or wood fires.[26] Similar to the ability of microwaves and infrared rays to heat materials, the word of God can produce a sense of burning. The two disciples going to Emmaus after the resurrection of Christ felt a burning in their hearts while the resurrected Christ opened the scriptures to them (Luke 24:32).

Infrared light is a light made up of electromagnetic energy. Its waves are shorter than microwaves but longer than visible light waves. Infrared light is invisible to the human eye. The human body naturally receives and emits this light. Objects that are not hot enough to produce visible light still release infrared energy. We cannot hide from the presence of God because God is omnipresent (is everywhere), and because the human body naturally receives and emits this light (infrared light), the couple could not hide from God (Psalm 139:7).

---

[26] Lumen, "Radiation," https://courses.lumenlearning.com/physics/chapter/14-7-radiation/.

## The Emission Spectrum and the Absorption Spectrum

There is a surprising analogy between the emission spectrum and absorption spectrum of electromagnetic radiation from natural light and the light that comes from God's light. Everybody absorbs and emits radiation at all frequencies in quantities that depend on its temperature. For example, this article's reader may be receiving radiation from the sun and radiating heat from it. This heat can be detected with an infrared camera. The scriptures say, "Neither do people light a lamp and put it under a bowl. Instead, they put it on its stand, and it gives light to everyone in the house" (Matthew 5:15–16).

## Nonionizing Electromagnetic Field

Nonionizing radiation includes the following electromagnetic fields:: radio waves, microwaves, and infrared radiation, including visible light. Shallow-frequency fields and static electric and magnetic fields also fall into this "nonionizing" category. Radiation composed of quanta of light without sufficient energy to break the molecular bonds is known as nonionizing radiation.

The believer whose faith is weak is analogous to nonionizing radiation, but we have to accept him (Matthew 26:40). Of all the seven electromagnetic spectra, radio waves, microwaves, and infrared waves are forms of nonionizing radiation.

The sources of human-generated electromagnetic fields that make up a critical part of industrial societies (through electricity, microwaves, and radiofrequency fields, for example) are at the end of the electromagnetic spectrum. They are of relatively long wavelengths and low frequencies, and they cannot break chemical bonds.

Nonionizing radiation constitutes, in general, the part of

the electromagnetic spectrum whose photon energy is too weak to break atomic bonds. But for those whose faith is weak, like nonionizing radiation, if they lack faith or wisdom, they can ask God, and he will give it to them (James 1:5).

"Non-ionizing radiation, even when high intensity, cannot cause ionization in a biological system."[27] This is similar to those who say, "Lord, Lord," believing that for doing this they will enter the kingdom of God. But only the one who does the will of the Father who is in heaven will enter the kingdom of God (Matthew 7:21).

It has been proven that such radiation can produce biological effects, such as heating, alteration of chemical reactions, and induction of electrical currents in tissues and cells. These biological effects are similar to the burning the disciples felt within their hearts when Jesus, the resurrected, opened the scriptures to them (Lucas 24:32).

## Risks in the Environment

The environment is saturated with radio frequencies. The entire population, to a greater or lesser extent, is subjected to high-frequency fields: television signals, radio signals (from FM and AM stations, amateur channels, channels used by taxis, firefighters, police, military, and so forth), telephone signals, Wi-Fi, radar, and so on. These fields pose a growing threat to health and nature. Such is the destructive power of these types of radiation that the arms industry has developed weapons that use microwaves to immobilize or eliminate people, as well as electromagnetic field inhibitors for use against hostile populations. "Its people defile the earth; they have disobeyed the laws, violated the statutes, and broken the everlasting covenant" (Isaiah 24:5).

There is an abundance of scientific writing about studies on

---

[27] Universidad Complutense Madrid, "Campos electromagnéticos y efectos biológicos," https://www.ucm.es/ima/campos-electromagneticos-y-efectos-biologicos.

radio frequencies and their effects on the exposed population's health. Radio and television stations and radar serve as examples of what to expect with the frequencies and powers used by mobile telephony. But these were ignored by public officials and, of course, by companies, allowing a microwave field to become widespread, affecting practically the entire world population. Analog telephony, the forerunner of digital telephony, uses signals like those used in radio and television. In contrast, digital telephony operates using pulsed microwaves remarkably like those used in radar. And the epidemiological literature on population exposure to radio, television, and radar radio frequencies years ago indicated there are risks of brain cancer, leukemia, and other types of tumors associated with such exposure, in addition to cardiac, neurological, and reproductive alterations in direct relation to the dose received. That is, the higher the dose, the more significant the increase in the risk percentage.

But there is hope for those who have faith in the Source (the Creator) of those electromagnetic fields and are overexposed to them. "When you pass through the waters, I will be with you, and when you pass through the rivers, they will not sweep over you. When you walk through the fire, you will not be burned; the flames will not set you ablaze" (Isaiah 43:2).

# CHAPTER 7

## The Son's Radiance of God's Glory Is Similar to the Electromagnetic Spectrum of Visible Light

———

The electromagnetic spectrum comprises the span of all electromagnetic radiation and consists of many subranges, commonly referred to as portions, such as visible light and ultraviolet radiation.

### Electromagnetic Radiation

Electromagnetic (EM) radiation is a form of energy that is all around us and takes many forms, such as (1) radio waves, (2) microwaves, (3) X-rays, and (4) gamma rays.

These four portions of the electromagnetic field are analogous to God as Light (Spirit). You cannot see them, but you can feel them.

And behold, the glory of the God of Israel was coming from the way of the east. And His voice was like the sound of many waters; and the earth shone with His glory. (Ezekiel 42:2)

Pay attention to Me, O My people, and give ear to Me, O My nation; For a law will go forth from Me, And I will set My justice for a light of the peoples. (Isaiah 51:4)

Therefore, I have hewn them in pieces by the prophets; I have slain them by the words of My mouth, And the judgments on you are like the light that goes forth. (Hosea 6:5)

Out of Zion, the perfection of beauty, God has shone forth. (Psalm 50:2)

Out of the brightness of his presence, clouds advanced, with hailstones and bolts of lightning. The LORD thundered from heaven, the voice of the Most High resounded. He shot his arrows and scattered the enemy; with great bolts of lightning, he routed them. (Psalm 18:12–14).

## Electromagnetic Spectrum

Quantum physics says, "The electromagnetic spectrum is the range of all types of electromagnetic radiation. The radiation that makes up the electromagnetic spectrum is composed of seven regions or portions: (1) radio waves, (2) microwaves, (3) infrared light, (4) visible light, (5) ultraviolet light, (6) X rays, (7) gamma rays."

Sunlight is a source of electromagnetic radiation visible in only a small portion of the electromagnetic spectrum. What can be seen with the naked eye of sunlight's radiation is white light. That white light is composed of the seven colors of the rainbow and can be seen through a prism.

A dispersive prism can break white light up into its constituent spectral colors (the colors of the rainbow). The incarnation of Jesus Christ is analogous to a prism that irradiates the Father's True Light.

> The true light that gives light to everyone was coming into the world. (John 1:9)

> The Son is the radiance of God's glory and the exact representation of his being, sustaining all things by his powerful word. (Hebrews 1:3)

The seven regions, or portions, of natural light's electromagnetic spectrum are analogous to the rainbow's seven colors. John saw one seated on a giant throne in heaven. A rainbow that shone like an emerald encircled the throne (Revelation 4:3).

## The Seven Spirits of God's True Light

Isaiah prophesied about the coming of Jesus Christ and said that seven spirits would rest in him. (Isaiah 12:2). In the Book of Revelation, John saw that the Lamb had seven horns and seven eyes, which were the seven spirits of God sent out into all the earth. (Revelation 5:6).

The scriptures attest to the many visible manifestations of God to humankind (epiphanies) that have come through the elements of nature, especially the fire that produces light and purifies. For example, "In the eyes of the children of Israel, the appearance of the glory of the LORD was like a consuming fire on the top of the mountain" (Deuteronomy 24:7).

I could quote many more texts with the referent of fire (light) linked to the manifestation of the Deity in men's affairs.

## Jesus, the Light of the World, the Purifying Fire Analogous to the Electromagnetic Spectrum's Visible Light

The visible spectrum is the region of the electromagnetic spectrum that the human eye can perceive. Electromagnetic radiation in this range of wavelengths is called "visible light," or simply "light." "The people living in darkness have seen a great light; on those living in the land of the shadow of death a light has dawned" (Matthew 4:16).

White light is a mixture of many different colors, each with a different frequency. White light can be split up into a spectrum of these colors using a prism, a triangular glass block. The regions of the electromagnetic spectrum are gamma rays, X-rays, ultraviolet radiation, the visible spectrum, microwaves, and radio frequencies.

Light refracts when it enters the prism. This means that light leaving the prism is spread out into its various colors, in a process called "dispersion."

No one has ever seen God, but the one and only Son, who is himself God and is in closest relationship with the Father, has made him known (John 1:18).

## Jesus Is Analogous to the Visible Light of the Electromagnetic Spectrum

The visible spectrum is the portion of the electromagnetic spectrum visible to the human eye. Electromagnetic radiation in this range of wavelengths is called "visible light," or simply "light." The Word became flesh and made his dwelling among us. We have seen his glory—the glory of the one and only Son, who came from the Father, full of grace and truth (John 1:14). Jesus said, "I am the light of the world. Whoever follows me will never walk in darkness but will have the light of life" (John 8:12).

When it comes to UV light, on the electromagnetic spectrum UV light falls between visible light and X-rays. This is then split into different UV light classifications: UVA, UVB, and UVC. These different UV light classifications have most recently been popularly deployed in air purification systems to effectively kill and remove microorganisms like bacteria, viruses, and mold spores from the air of an indoor environment.[28]

Analogous to the UV purification light, if we walk in the light, as he is in the light, we have fellowship with one another. The blood of Jesus, his Son, purifies us from all sin. (1 John 1:7). He will sit as a refiner and purifier of silver; he will purify the Levites and refine them like gold and silver. Then the LORD will have men who will bring offerings in righteousness. (Malachi 3:3). He is the image of the invisible God, the firstborn of all creation (Colossians 1:15).

The scriptures mention Jesus in many biblical texts both in the Old and New Testaments, where the Messiah, Jesus Christ, is linked to the referent of fire and light.

More than five hundred years BC, the prophet Isaiah prophesied about the coming of Christ and cataloged him as the "light" that shines in the darkness. Seeing the condition of the people, the prophet Isaiah called it spiritual darkness caused by the evil, fear, and discouragement experienced by the people at that time when the Assyrians attacked the land of Zebulon and the land of Naphtali. "Distressed and hungry, they will roam through the land; when they are famished, they will become enraged and, looking upward, will curse their king and their God. Then they

---

[28] Amanda Wooley, "Understanding UV Light Technology in Air Purifiers," EnviroKlenz, December 26, 2019, https://enviroklenz.com/uv-light-technology-air-purifiers#:.

will look toward the earth and see only distress and darkness and fearful gloom, and they will be thrust into utter darkness" (Isaiah 8:21–22).

Isaiah goes on to prophesy about the light that would come and shine upon them: "Nevertheless, there will be no more gloom for those who were in distress. In the past, he humbled the land of Zebulon and the land of Naphtali. Still, in the future, he will honor Galilee of the nations, by way of the Sea, beyond the Jordan— The people walking in darkness have seen a great light; on those living in the land of deep darkness, a light has dawned" (Isaiah 9:1–2).

In Isaiah 42:6, God says that he, the Lord, has called him in righteousness through the prophet. He will hold him with his hand and make it a covenant for the nations and light for the Gentiles, open the eyes of the blind, free the captives from prison, and release from the dungeon those who sit in darkness. He will also make him a light for the Gentiles, that his salvation may reach to the ends of the earth (Isaiah 49:6).

And more than five hundred years later, the New Testament writer Luke links and relates the beginning of Jesus's ministry to the prophecy of Isaiah when he stands in the temple to read the scroll and he reads his prophetic mission that says, "The Spirit of the Lord is on me; because he has anointed me to proclaim good news to the poor. He has sent me to proclaim freedom for the prisoners and recovery of sight for the blind, to set the oppressed free, to proclaim the year of the lord's favor" (Luke 4:18–19).

# CHAPTER 8

## Analogies Between Quantum Physics Laws and the Teachings of Jesus

Light is a form of energy emitted by luminous bodies; we perceive light through the sense of sight.

In the same way, let your light shine before others, that they may see your good deeds and glorify your Father in heaven. (Matthew 5:16)

> The true light that gives light to everyone was coming into the world. He was in the world, and though the world was made through him, the world did not recognize him. (John 1:9)

> In Him was life, and that life was the light of men1. I, the light, have come into the world … (John 1:3–4)

> When Jesus spoke again to the people, he said, "I am the light of the world. Whoever follows me

will never walk in darkness but will have the light of life." (John 8:12)

Yet I am writing you a new command; its truth is seen in him and you, because the darkness is passing, and the true light is already shining. (1 John 2:8)

Then Jesus told them, "You are going to have the light just a little while longer. Walk while you have the light before darkness overtakes you. Whoever walks in the dark does not know where they are going." (John 12:35)

Once the light has been produced, it will keep traveling in a straight line until it hits something else. Shadows are evidence of light traveling in straight lines. An object blocks light so that it cannot reach the surface, where we see the shadow. Light fills up all of the space before it hits the object, but the whole region between the object and the surface is in shadow. Shadows do not appear completely dark because there is still some light reaching the surface that has been reflected off other objects. Once the light has hit another surface or particles, it is then absorbed, reflected (bounced off), scattered (bounced off in all directions), and refracted (its direction and speed changed). "Where can I go from your Spirit? Where can I flee from your presence? If I go up to the heavens, you are there; if I make my bed in the depths, you are there. If I rise on the wings of the dawn, if I settle on the far side of the sea, even there your hand will guide me, your right hand will hold me fast" (Psalm 7:10).

## Quantum Physics and the Scriptures

In essence, quantum physics is the study of matter and energy at small and nanoscopic levels, beginning within nuclei, atoms, and molecules. Modern science declares that quantum particles (light packets of the particle wave) form atoms. These atoms form molecules, and molecules form objects. All we can see is these quantum particles. What makes these quantum particles so unique is that they do not behave according to the known laws of Newtonian physics and Descartes's physics, making them more of a series of probabilities rather than something we can define and observe and measure objectively with our physical senses.

Quantum Physics says: "Everything we can see is made up of things we cannot see—particles called quanta." The Scriptures say: "By faith, we understand that the universe was formed at God's command so that what is seen was not made out of what was visible." (Hebrews 11:3). Quantum Physics say: "What you see is made of that which is not seen. As you go deeper and deeper into the workings of the atom, you see that there is nothing there—just energy waves. An atom is an invisible force field, a kind of miniature tornado that emits waves of electrical energy." The Scriptures say: "By the word of the LORD the heavens were made, their starry host by the breath of his mouth" (Psalm 33:6).

Quantum Physics says: "There are no empty spaces in the universe; everything is permeated with light." The Scriptures say: "If I said: Surely the darkness will cover me; even the darkness will not be dark to you; the night will shine like the day, for darkness is as light to you. and the night shines like the day; Dusk is the same as light." (Psalm 139:11–12).

Quantum Physics says: "The magnetic field of the quantum cannot be seen, but it is a powerful force." The Scriptures say: "By his power he churned up the sea; by his wisdom he cut Rahab to pieces." (Job 26:7-14) - "For the LORD, your God is a consuming fire, although you cannot see Him, is a jealous God" (Philippians 4:13).

Quantum Physics says: "All electromagnetic radiation propagated in waveforms in any space can travel through a vacuum at a speed of approximately three hundred thousand kilometers per second." The Scriptures say: "For as lightning that comes from the east is visible even in the west, so will be the coming of the Son of Man" (Matthew 24:27).

Are you feeling fear or anxiety? Are you frightened? Are you worried that something undesirable will occur or happen to you? Are you unwilling or reluctant to do something for fear of the consequences? If so, you are taken by the emotion of Adam's inheritance of fear. The scriptures say, "The LORD is my light and my salvation— whom shall, I fear? The LORD is the stronghold of my life— of whom shall I be afraid?" (Psalm 27:1).

# CHAPTER 9

## Analogies between Quantum Physics Laws and Jesus Christ's Gospel Teachings

There are interesting analogies between the laws of quantum physics and the teachings of the gospel of Jesus Christ. Here are some examples of these analogies:

**Black Body Radiation Is Analogous to the Christian Believer**

A black body is a theoretical or ideal object that absorbs all the light and the radiant energy that falls on it.

> The people living in darkness have seen a great light; on those living in the land of the shadow of death a light has dawned. (Matthew 4:16)

Neither do people light a lamp and put it under a bowl. Instead, they put it on its stand, and it gives light to everyone in the house. In the same way, let your light shine before others, that they may see your good deeds and glorify your Father in heaven. (Matthew 5:15–16)

For God, who said, "Let light shine out of darkness," made his light shine in our hearts to give us the light of the knowledge of God's glory displayed in the face of Christ." (2 Corinthians 4:6)

When Jesus spoke again to the people, he said, "I am the light of the world. Whoever follows me will never walk in darkness but will have the light of life." (John 8:12)

Despite its name, a black body emits light and constitutes an idealized physical system for studying the emission of electromagnetic radiation. The scriptures say, "In the same way, let your light shine before others, that they may see your good deeds and glorify your Father in heaven," (Matthew 5:16).

## Electromagnetic Radiation Is Analogous to the Black Body (the Believer)

Everybody emits energy in the form of electromagnetic waves. This radiation, which is emitted even in a vacuum, grows more intense as the emitter's temperature increases. The scriptures say, "The LORD bless you and keep you; the LORD make his face shine on you and be gracious to you" (Jeremiah 6:24–25).

The radiant energy emitted by a body at room temperature is scarce and corresponds to wavelengths lower than those of visible light (that is, of lower frequencies, such as those of infrared light, or frequencies even lower). The scriptures say, "Because you are lukewarm, and neither cold nor hot, am I to spit you out of my mouth" (Revelation 3:15–16).

Raising the temperature increases the energy emitted, but the energy is then emitted at shorter wavelengths; this is due to the change of color of a body when it is heated. Bodies do not emit with equal intensity at all frequencies. The scriptures say, "If anyone builds on this foundation using gold, silver, costly stones, wood, hay or straw, their work will be shown for what it is because the Day will bring it to light. It will be revealed with fire, and the fire will test the quality of each person's work" (1 Corinthians 3:12–13).

## Quantum Chromodynamics and the Chromodynamics of the Four Horses of the Apocalypse

The legendary four horsemen of the Apocalypse are, for many, one of the most talked-about mysteries in the Bible. About two thousand years ago, the apostle John compiled the details of his writing. Since then, ordinary scholars and believers have wondered what these four horsemen of the Apocalypse mean and represent. Much has been written concerning these four horsemen, much of it misapplied to struggles between nations and potential conquerors, as well as to the horrors of tribulation under the antichrist. Currently, the Book of Revelation is not concerned with world kingdoms and world empires, or wars, struggles, famines, and pestilences, except that they are tied to spiritual affairs of the children of God. The Book of Revelation, as I have repeatedly pointed out, is a spiritual revelation, this being the revelation of Jesus Christ. Thus, the four horsemen and the four horses represent, like the figures in the rest of the book, aspects of a growing revelation or unveiling of Jesus Christ in and through our bodies. These are spiritual realities felt and known only "in spirit and by spirit."

The Four Horsemen of the Apocalypse are among the most significant of the great symbols in the Word of God, because they gives us the key to the processing of God within us. When we can have full meaning and understanding of how the scriptures speak of horses to teach us spiritual truths, we can gain an appreciation for Biblical symbolism. The Bible is not written in one style like just another ordinary book. It has its own method of presenting spiritual realities through picturesque symbols, which is the language of the spirit communicated to the mind of humankind, wisdom expressed in terms understandable by people in all times and in different parts of the world and with different degrees of spiritual development.

The four horses and their riders present a picture of God's dealings, stripping, purging, processing, imparting, and transforming, by which we are reduced to God. A fast, powerful, and irresistible ruin of deception visits our outer world of consciousness, human identity, and our inner being. As the seals of self-revelation are opened, we notice that what comes to the surface represents what is within us—the power of life, symbolized as horses. These are figures of great strength, power, and self-improvement (Zechariah 10: 3).

How can someone be placed in a position of authority and power in the kingdom? He will cleanse the sons of Levi, the kings, and the priests of his kingdom; disqualify those who cannot be trusted to do the Father's will; and fully cooperate in the administration of his grace and glory. In this important hour, the ways of Babylon and all the resources of the flesh, centered on the carnal church systems, are being thoroughly purged; the attributes of the carnal mind being cleansed; all selfishness being burned; and all desire to make a name for ourselves or to gather men around ourselves, rather than for Christ, being consumed.

Thank goodness he is doing it. The horsemen are riding through our land.

Translated into spiritual language, the four horses and their riders present an image of Christ making war against the flesh, the intention of the flesh, and the natural human. The four horsemen portray war, calamities, destruction, and death inflicted on the carnal forms of humankind. These four horses are the warhorses of God—manifestations of him "who is called Faithful and True and in righteousness he judges and fights" (Revelation 19:11). They are sent to our personal lands to destroy all the enemies of God's law in us. They destroy the usurper, the serpent of the intention of the flesh, the will of the flesh, the desires of the flesh, the emotions of the flesh, the works of the flesh, and the religious claim of the flesh. In short, these horsemen conquer and destroy everything they encounter with their strength, the activity of the flesh. So do not be surprised at the fiery ordeal that has come on you to test you, as though something strange were happening to you. But rejoice inasmuch as you participate in the sufferings of Christ, so that you may be overjoyed when his glory is revealed (1 Peter 4:12–13).

## The Law of Displacement

The law of displacement shows how the energy density curve shifts as the temperature changes over a black body.

The colors of electromagnetic radiation emitted by a black body in thermal equilibrium at a defined temperature define the thermal degree emitted by the light. The maximum point of heat emitted by the color red is 3,500 K; the color yellow is 5,000 K, and green is 5,500 K. $K$ is the temperature of the sun's photosphere—about 5,800 Kelvin.

Peter says, "Dear friends, do not be surprised at the fiery ordeal that has come on you to test you, as though something strange were happening to you … In all this, you greatly rejoice, though now for a little while you may have had to suffer grief in all kinds of trials. These have come so that the proven genuineness of your faith—of greater worth than gold, which perishes even though refined by fire—may result in praise, glory, and honor when Jesus Christ is revealed …" (1 Peter 4:12, 6, 7). Their work will be shown for what it is because the day will bring it to light. It will be revealed with fire, and the fire will test the quality of each person's work (1 Corinthians 3:13).

## The Four Horsemen of the Apocalypse

The four horses of the Apocalypse represent a parallelism with the action of the electromagnetic field. Light's force radiates onto objects or subatomic particles. The law of displacement shows how the energy density curve shifts as the temperature changes over a black body.

The law of displacement is a parallel of the four horses of the Apocalypse with the displacement of the power of the Holy Spirit in the believer in different trials for the purification and perfection of the body of Christ, the church.

In Revelation 5, the risen slain Lamb takes the scroll from the right hand of the one who sat at the throne, and the elders tell John not to cry because the Lion of the Tribe of Judah, not the meek Lamb, would open the scroll and its seven seals. When the Lamb who had been slain went and took the scroll from the right hand of he who sat at the throne, many angels, numbering thousands upon thousands, and ten thousand times ten thousand, began to say in a loud voice: "Worthy is the Lamb, who was slain, to receive power and wealth and wisdom and strength and honor and glory and praise. Every creature in heaven and on earth and under the earth and on the sea, and all that is in them, saying: To him who sits on the throne and to the Lamb be praise and honor and glory and power, forever and ever!" The four living creatures said, "Amen," and the elders bowed down and worshiped. (Revelation 5).

## The White Horse

"I watched as the Lamb opened the first of the seven seals. Then I heard one of the four living creatures say in a voice like thunder, "Come!" I looked, and there before me was a **white** horse! Its rider held a bow, and he was given a crown, and he rode out as a conqueror bent on conquest" (Revelation 6:1). It should not be difficult for anyone to understand that the horseman riding a white horse, holding a bow, and wearing a crown, is none other than the forerunner, our Lord Jesus Christ, this time coming not as the humble Lamb but as the Lion of the Tribe of Judah. He comes as a conqueror bent on conquest. He rides a white horse, and the color white contains the seven colors of white light. This means that of the four horses, this horse is the strongest.

And so Jesus Christ, astride the snow-white horse, puts himself in a position where he is perpetually celebrating a victory. His march is a victorious march. His movements are always successful. His plans are fulfilled, and his campaigns unfold in the breeze of the flags of triumph. Jesus Christ goes forth as a conqueror, and he does so with great speed and power. The action in which he engages requires the most extraordinary power, even the power of the Spirit, and his movements are energized with tremendous force.

There are things in your life that seem to be impossible and invincible. The white horse's rider comes with the bow (the force) to shoot the arrow, the Word of God, with the power of the Holy Spirit directed at the mind and the heart, to make the carnal die in us. That is the inheritance of the transgenerational trauma of the old Adam. This is the heritage of problems with attitudes, fears, desires, emotions, circumstances, weaknesses, habits, and defects that only Jesus Christ can throw out by the power of his Word. As he said when he came for the first time, "Do not suppose that I have come to bring peace to the earth. I did not come to bring peace but a sword. For I have come to turn a man against his father, a daughter against her mother, a daughter-in-law against her mother-in-law— a man's enemies will be the members of his own household" (Matthew 10:34–36).

The rider of the first white horse is Christ himself, who comes not as the Lamb whom they spat upon, outraged, and killed, but as the Lamb who was slain, raised, resurrected, and, on the third day, ascended to heaven, where he sat victorious at the right hand of the Father—the Lamb who overcame the grave and death, took the book from the Father's right hand and was willing to come as a Conqueror to open the seals of the book. Now he is coming as the Lion of the Tribe of Judah to open the book that has been sealed since the time of Daniel (Daniel 12:4).

## The Red Horse

> When the Lamb opened the second seal, I heard the second living creature say, "Come!" Then another horse came out, a fiery **red** one. Its rider was given the power to take peace from the earth and to make people kill each other. To him was given a large sword. (Revelation 6:3–4)

> For the word of God is alive and active, sharper than any double-edged sword, it penetrates even to dividing soul and spirit, joints and marrow; it judges the thoughts and attitudes of the heart. (Hebrews 4:12)

"Is not my word like fire," declares the LORD?
(Jeremiah 23:29)

When Christ enters our land like the red horse, he removes
the peace from our land; that is, he disturbs our comfort zone.
Once the Spirit of God quickens us, once we awaken to our true
identities, once we stand up as new creations, we are no longer
comfortable with the things of the old Adam. Within us we have
awakened new desires, new possibilities, new hopes, new ways of
thinking, new perceptions of reality, a new understanding, a new
nature, a new mind, a new heart. Now we are not comfortable with
the things that we were comfortable with before. In the old Adam,
we were at ease in worldly environments, carnal understandings,
and carnal activities; But now that the mind of Christ has been
awakened in us, peace has fled from our land, from our souls.
What this means is that all the peace, pleasure, and joy of the
earthly, natural, carnal life is taken away. The more we are
awakened to the beauty and glory of life in the spirit, the more
our earthly condition is perceived as a vile abomination. The red
horse carries a sword that causes division between the soul and
the spirit, between the natural life and the heavenly life. A burning
sensation is also kindled within us; it is the purging fire that will
begin to cleanse our earth of all despicable and carnal things.

**The Black Horse**

"When the Lamb opened the third seal, I heard the third
living creature say, 'Come!' I looked, and there before me was a
**black** horse! Its rider was holding a pair of scales in his hand. Then
I heard what sounded like a voice among the four living creatures,
saying, 'Two pounds of wheat for a day's wages, and six pounds of
barley for a day's wages, and do not damage the oil and the wine!'
(Revelation 6:5–6). The black horse is analogous to the black body

of quantum physics. I previously stated that a black body is a theoretical object that absorbs all the light and all the radiant energy that falls on it, constituting an idealized physical system by which to study the emission of electromagnetic radiation.

When the black horse gallops over our land, in a fashion similar to the black body of quantum physics, we absorb all the light of the Word that the rider of the white horse radiates on us. "He does not light a lamp and hides under a table but puts it on it and illuminates everyone at home" (Luke 11:33).

In the gospel, the righteousness of God is revealed by faith, as it is written: "BUT THE JUST BY FAITH WILL LIVE" (Romans 1:17). Once the black horse begins to travel our land, we analogous become the black body of the quantum realm, and we absorb all the light of the Word and reflect it in the divine justice represented by the pair of scales and the wine and the oil, "not altering the scales or adulterating the wine or oil. The Lord detests dishonest scales, but accurate weights find favor with him." (Proverbs 11:1).

## The Green Horse

"When the Lamb opened the fourth seal, I heard the voice of the fourth living creature say, 'Come!' I looked, and there before me was a **pale horse**! Its rider was named Death, and Hades was following close behind him. They were given power over a fourth of the earth to kill by sword, famine and plague, and by the wild beasts of the earth" (Revelation 6:7,8).[29] There is a special meaning that fits the description of the fourth horseman—the one whose name is Death—and Hades followed him. Death and hell are especially linked in Revelation. And since Christ came and took away death (2 Timothy 1:10) and destroyed the one who had the power of death—that is, the devil (Hebrews 2:14)—he now confidently proclaims, "I am the one who lives, and was dead;

---

[29] *Strong's* G5515 gives "pale horse" as having the meaning "green."

and behold, I live forever and ever, and I have the keys of hell and death" (Revelation 1:18). And since Christ now possesses both hell and death because he has overcome them and taken them for himself, neither can dwell anywhere except by his authority.

The King James Bible identifies this fourth horse as a "pale" horse. The translators had difficulty with the word "green" because this horse brings "death, hell, plagues." They could not understand the use of "green" concerning death and hades, so they used the word "pale." Other translators use "pale ash," "sickly green," "livid," "ash-colored," and so forth to describe something that is sickly, hellish, or dead.

If we put the color "green" in the context of this work, the green color is the fourth of the seven colors that appears in a rainbow. The green color belongs to the fourth portion (visual light) of the electromagnetic spectrum. The fourth step of Moses's tabernacle is the door called the Truth, which leads to the Holy Place.

There are three doors in the tabernacle of Moses: (1) the tabernacle's door at the entrance (the Way); (2) the door leading to the Holy Place (the Truth); and (3) the door leading to the Most Holy Place (the Life).

Thus, the biblical text reads, "I am **(the way)** and **(the truth)** and **(the life)**. No one comes to the Father except through me" (John 14: 6, emphasis added).

The door at the entrance to the Holy Place (the Truth) is like the door at the entrance to the tabernacle(the Way). But there is a difference. Of the Way in the tabernacle's entry, the Bible states, "All the posts around the courtyard are to **have silver bands and hooks**, and bronze bases ..." (Exodus 27:16–17). The door (the Truth) leading to the Holy Place has "five posts with hooks for them. They overlaid the tops of the posts and their **bands with gold** and made their five bases of bronze" (Exodus 36:37–38).

So the fourth horse, the green horse, correlates with the fourth rainbow color, the fourth portion of the electromagnetic spectrum, visual light, the fourth step in the tabernacle of Moses, and the door leading to the Holy Place (the Truth).

The difference between the door at the Tabernacle's entrance (the Way) and the door leading to the Holy Place (the Truth) is that the Way, has *four posts with silver bands and hooks*, and the Truth has *five posts with their tops and their bands overlaid with gold*. In both doors, their bases are made of bronze.

There is a point in a black body where the color green changes to blue. This quantum leap from green to blue is due to the behavior of photons' nanoparticles. Scientists could not keep studying the matter with the knowledge and the old instruments of Newton's and Descartes's classical physics. They had to discover new ways and new devices to study matter.

The green horse brings death that is similar to the death of the old Adamic inheritance of sin in us. This is analogous to being on the fourth step of the tabernacle of Moses, where we stand in front of the door leading to the Holy Place (the Truth). But to go beyond that door, one must be filled with the Holy Spirit, as on the day of Pentecost, and become a "new creature"—be "born again," as Jesus told Nicodemus. That is why the door leading to the Holy Place has five posts with their top and their bands overlaid with gold, instead of four posts with silver bands and hooks like the door at the entrance of the tabernacle (the Way). Here on the fourth step of the tabernacle, the five poles are overlaid with gold; in the first door, the Way, the four poles are overlaid with silver. In the seven electromagnetic portions of the electromagnetic spectrum, the red horse, the black horse, and the green horse are analogous to the weak forces: radio waves, microwaves, and infrared rays. The fifth, six, and seventh seals are analogous to the strong forces: ultraviolet rays, X-rays, and gamma rays. These rays can damage the DNA and penetrate deep inside the body, but if used correctly, they can be of great benefit in healing.

These weak forces and strong forces have a parallelism with Job's being tested for faithfulness to God. Satan questioned Job's faithfulness to God because God had blessed Job with family and riches. Satan told God to strike everything Job had, stating that Job would then surely curse God to his face. In a noticeably short time, Job received four messages, each bearing separate news that his livestock, servants, and ten children had all died because of invaders and natural catastrophes. Job tore his clothes and shaved his head in mourning, but he still blessed God and said, "Naked I came from my mother's womb, and naked I will depart. The LORD gave and the LORD has taken away; may the name of the LORD be praised." (Job 1:1–20).

Satan appeared in heaven for the second time, and the LORD said to Satan, "Have you considered my servant Job? There is no one on earth like him; he is blameless and upright, a man who fears God and shuns evil. And he still maintains his integrity, though you incited me against him to ruin him without any reason" (Job 2:3). Satan replied to God, "Skin for skin! A man will give all he has for his own life. But now stretch out your hand and strike his flesh and bones, and he will surely curse you to your face" (Job 2:4).

Suddenly Job was afflicted with a horrible skin disease. His wife told him to curse God and give up and die, but Job refused, struggling to accept his circumstances. Now Job was suffering the test in his own flesh.

In the first test, which is analogous to the quantum weak force, Job suffered the test on the outside. He was a mere spectator in the spectacle and praised the Lord anyway. In the second test, he suffered in his own flesh with ulcers all over his body. After this, Job opened his mouth and cursed the day of his birth. He said,

"May the day of my birth perish, and the night that said, 'A boy is conceived!'" (Job 3:1–3).

In a way analogous to the electromagnetic spectrum's strong forces, Job started cursing, although he never denied God.

*Strong's Concordance* gives the meaning of the Greek word root for "*kloros*" simply as "green." The actual form of the word used in the text is "kloros." The best key to discovering the meaning of any word is its use. This Greek word appears in only three places in the New Testament. Let us see how the word is translated there and what its obvious meaning from its use is. When Jesus was preparing to multiply the loaves and the fishes to feed the five thousand, "… he commanded them to make them all sit down in groups on the green [kloros] grass" (Mark 6:39).

The slain Lamb of God, the Lion of the Tribe of Judah, the Root of David, has triumphed. He came on a white horse. He can open the scroll and its seven seals. He rode out as a conqueror bent on conquest. Jesus, the Word, said, "I am the Light of the World" (John 8:12).

Jesus as the Light of the World is analogous to natural light. Natural light is white light, a combination of all colors in the color spectrum. It has all the rainbow's colors. One can see the colors through a prism, and like a prism, the white horse dispersed the various colors, such as the red horse. Its rider was given power to take peace from the earth and to make people kill each other. To him was given a large sword. When Jesus was teaching his message here on the earth, he said, "Do not suppose that I have come to bring peace to the earth. I did not come to bring peace, but a sword" (Matthew 10:34). Put to death therefore, whatever belongs to your earthly nature, such as sexual immorality, impurity, lust, evil desire and greed, which is idolatry. Because of these, the wrath of God is coming. You used to walk in these ways in the life you once lived. (Colossians 3:5–7).

# CHAPTER 10

## Analogies between the Salvation Plan and Quantum Physics Laws

---

It seems logical that the Creator, who created humankind in his image and likeness, has thought of an intelligent design—a tiny molecule that allows the development of all living beings (DNA). More surprising still, it seems even more logical to us that by creating humankind in his image and likeness, in that same DNA molecule, he added a code with information for the development of a neurophysiological support, the brain, which makes humankind superior to the rest of the animals created and gives them the ability to relate to their Creator. With this mechanism, humans know, reason, think, and, most distinctively, have, in addition to the five natural bodily senses, "the sense of spiritual perception," with which humankind can choose between good and evil, to choose between what suits them or not (ethics) and keeps them spiritually linked with the Creator.

Through the power of thought and the Word in action, everything created was made. Likewise, humans create and act with thought, knowledge, reasoning, and, even more so, by "the sense of spiritual perception" and not by the instinct and the drives of Darwin's five senses of natural human, believing in evolution instead of Creation.

By transgressing the supreme law, the man realized his true tragic existence, detachment from his Creator, and creation. When he recognized that he was naked and knew himself to be mortal like other created beings and that at some unknown moment death would overcome him, fear overtook him. "I heard your voice in the garden, and I was afraid because I was naked, and I hid" (Genesis 3:10).

humankind's disobedience had broken the balance of peace, tranquility, and harmony between God, humankind, and the entire creation. Now humankind was overcome by the "fear" of danger and death, which was not codified in the original human DNA. Now, without waiting for it, a series of uncontrolled physiological reactions were triggered inside humankind that humankind could not handle; humans now felt only the instinct to stand up and fight or flee from threatening danger. They chose to flee. From then on, they began to feel the emotion of fear that at any moment, death would surprise them, with no other choice.

The stress produced by this state of alert continuously in the body produces cortisol, and at the same time, owing to its short duration, it degrades and produces more free radicals in the blood, thus generating all kinds of diseases: Alzheimer's, cancer tumors, neuronal diseases, and other disorders that afflict humans to this day, not to mention depression and anxiety.

## Epigenetic

We are all have registered in the genome of our DNA the trauma of fear. For the first time, genes in Adam's DNA were epigenetically marked by the "fear" factor.[30] In epigenetics, external factors, such as environment, climate, beverages, and toxic foods; internal factors, such as strong emotions, thoughts, and beliefs; and the stress caused by prolonged fear produce epigenetic marks in the DNA's genome. An event that causes stress in the past may or may not activate in subsequent situations, such as an event producing post-traumatic stress disorder (PTSD). The emotion of fear, the mechanism that unleashes fear, is found in both people and animals, in the brain, specifically in the limbic system, which is responsible for regulating emotions, fighting, flight, the avoidance of pain, and, in general, all conservational functions of the individual and the species. This system constantly reviews (even during sleep) all the information that is received through the senses, and it does so through the structure called the cerebral amygdala, which controls the basic emotions, such as fear and affection, and is responsible for locating the source of the danger. When the amygdala has activated, the sensation of fear and anxiety is triggered, and its response can be fight or flight—a confrontation or a retreat.

## The Word of God Modifies DNA Marked with the Stain of the Spirit of Disobedience and the Fear of Death

> Therefore, just as sin entered the world through one man, and death through sin, and in this

---

[30] A gene is the basic physical and functional unit of heredity. Genes, which are made up of DNA, act as instructions to make molecules called proteins. In humans, genes vary in size from a few hundred DNA bases to more than 2 million bases. The Human Genome Project has estimated that humans have between 20,000 and 25,000 genes. Every person has two copies of each gene, one inherited from each parent. Most genes are the same in all people, but a small number (less than 1 percent of the total) are slightly different between people. Alleles are forms of the same gene with small differences in their sequence of DNA bases. These small differences contribute to each person's unique physical features. See ghr.nlm.nih.gov/primer/basics/gene.

way, death came to all people because all sinned. (Romans 5:12)

Although you wash yourself with soap and use an abundance of cleansing powder, the stain of your guilt is still before me. (Jeremiah 2:22)

The Word, the Light of this World, our Lord Jesus Christ, came to cleanse us—to purify us from the stain of sin "that dwells in our limbs" (at the center of each one of the billions of cells in our bodies) as a result of the "transgenerational trauma"[31] of fear to danger and death.

## The Transgenerational Genetic Memory

The fear suffered by Adam left epigenetic marks in the genome of his DNA, and these were transferred by genetic inheritance to subsequent generations (transgenerational trauma). Transgenerational genetic memory is a concept that describes the transfer of history marked in the genetic material of an individual or a species; this includes knowledge, skills, and traumas experienced throughout life by that individual or species or by

---

[31] The biological system comes into play when you cannot escape a threat, if you believe that you will die, or if you perceive that there is no end to what is happening. In this case, the body gets signals to slow down or shut down (the immobilization response). Recovery from immobilization takes significantly longer, and having good trauma therapy and social support, as well as getting exercise, is important. Studies of second-generation children of holocaust survivors reveal that children of mothers with PTSD are more likely to develop PTSD, as differentiated from children whose fathers had PTSD, suggesting the possible influence of genetics as differentiated from environmental influence. Twin studies also reveal a greater prevalence of PTSD among trauma survivors who also had a twin with PTSD, further reinforcing a genetic model. While more research is needed to tease apart the nature vs. nurture debate, results strongly suggest that there may be an epigenetic component to the transgenerational transmission of trauma. See http://drarielleschwartz.com.

that individual's or species's ancestors. The disobedience of having eaten the forbidden fruit not only produced a change in the couple, and through modification in DNA genetics, that memory of fear and that stress that this disobedience to the supreme law caused to them, having eaten the forbidden fruit of the Tree of Knowledge of Good and Evil, survived into the subsequent generations through genetic inheritance.

The transgression removed humankind from the garden, from communion with the Creator, from their knowledge, and from their science and wisdom, and left them, like the animals of Darwin, randomly guided by their instinctual drives. With the "transgression," DNA was altered—its genome, not its sequence—and epigenetic marks emerged that would modify its expression. Those epigenetic words, distorted and confused, spoken by the snake to the woman, tinged with irony and half-truths, brought confusion and doubt into the couple's mind. The man began to think and act according to his own thoughts, not those of his Creator. "'For my thoughts are not your thoughts, neither are your ways my ways,' declares the LORD. 'As the heavens are higher than the earth, so are my ways'" (Isaiah 55:8).

Discarding the words of the Creator, humankind lost all that information of the mysteries and the wisdom and the science of God, and 80 percent of their DNA became "junk," as some scientists term it.[32]

## Genetic Modification through Music and Words

Many genes in the original DNA created by God at the beginning of his Creation were marked and blocked after the

[32] Wojciech Makalowski, "What Is Junk DNA, and What Is It Worth?" Scientific American. February 12, 2007. https://www.scientificamerican.com/article/what-is-junk-dna-and-what/.

"fall of man" by environmental, external, and internal epigenetic factors.[33] But thanks to the Word of God, which takes away the sins of the world, we no longer have to be enslaved by our inheritance of sin, because "the Word of God can modify our DNA."[34]

> He took the sin away and cast it into the depths of the sea. You will again have compassion on us; you will tread our sins underfoot and hurl all our iniquities into the depths of the sea. (Micah 7:19)

## Music Can Modify DNA

Recent studies have discovered that the vibration of music's "sound waves" can modify DNA.[35] Also, the vibration of words can alter or modify DNA.[36] Remember the melodies performed by David in the scriptures; when playing his instrument, he relieved the symptoms of the mental and spiritual disturbance that afflicted King Saul. There is also the "creative word," such as the one that created each time the Creator issued it, or such as the

---

[33] Scientists have made some incredible new discoveries on how our minds can literally affect our biology, especially through the study of epigenetics, the branch of science that looks at how inherited changes of phenotype (appearance) or gene expression are caused by mechanisms other than changes in the underlying DNA sequence. Instead of looking at DNA as the only factor controlling our biology, scientists are also looking at what's actually *controlling* the DNA, which includes our thoughts. We receive genetic instructions from our DNA, passed down through generations, but the environment we live in can also make genetic changes. See http://www.collective-evolution.com/.

[34] *"Las palabras pueden modificar el AND - https://absolum.org/ciencia_adn_ palabras.htm#:~*

[35] See the works of Masaru Emoto on how music can modify the structure of water molecules.

[36] One can simply use words and sentences of the human language! This, too, has been experimentally proven! Living DNA substance (in living tissue, not in vitro) will always react to language-modulated laser rays and even to radio waves if the proper frequencies are being used. See http://www.collective-evolution.com.

other word of healing from Jesus about the servant of a Roman centurion: "*Go, and* as you believed, be done to you. And his servant was healed at that same hour ..." (Matthew 8:13).

According to scientific experiments, the sound waves of music and speech can deactivate or activate information contained in the DNA genome, offering endless open possibilities for genetic memory. So genes of the original DNA, as it was created, have been marked and blocked epigenetically by discordant music and ill-intentioned words, and transmitted genetically to humanity by the transgenerational trauma that has caused fears, phobias, mental disorders, diseases, plagues, wars, and death throughout human history. Also, that transgenerational trauma keeps us busy and stressed and creates false needs and endless diseases so that we never have time to connect with the Creator.

If in that 20 percent or 30 percent of our DNA is the instructional code of our being, just as we are, imagine what is in the other 70 or 80 percent that is blocked by the epigenetics in the "junk" DNA! As many scientists say, being ignorant of the Word leads us every day to act worse than or the same as Darwin's animals. "Is not my word like fire, says the Lord, and like a hammer that breaks the stone?" (Jeremiah 23:29).

An article published in the magazine *Urban Planetarium*, "The Power of the Word," tells us that the Russian biophysicist and molecular biologist Pjotr Garjajev and his colleagues explored the vibratory behavior of DNA. "Living chromosomes work like solitonic /holographic computers using laser radiation from endogenous DNA."[37] That means that one can simply use words and sentences from human language to influence DNA or reprogram it.

The article goes on to say that the spiritual and religious masters of antiquity have known, for thousands of years, that our bodies can be programmed through language, words, and thinking. Remember the words that Moses told the people when

---

[37] (see footnote 37)

he gave them the law in the wilderness: "Love the LORD your God with all your heart and with all your soul and with all your strength. These commandments that I give you today are to be in your hearts. Impress them on your children. Talk about them when you sit at home and when you walk along the road, when you lie down and when you get up. Tie them as symbols on your hands and bind them on your foreheads. Write them on the doorframes of your houses and your gates" (Deuteronomy 6:5–9).

The article goes on to say that 90 percent of "junk DNA" stores information. "Imagine a library that instead of archiving thousands of books only saves the alphabet common to all books, then, when you request the information of a certain book, the alphabet gathers everything contained in its pages and makes it available to us. This opens the doors to an even greater mystery, says the author: That the real library would be outside our bodies in some unknown place in the cosmos and that the DNA would be in permanent communication with this universal reservoir of knowledge.

## The Word of God as Fire

The man was left without the wisdom and knowledge of his Creator, without his image, without his Spirit, and without the full knowledge of what is good or bad and of what is convenient or not for him. Instead of being guided by the Spirit of the Creator, humankind began to be guided by impulses of the unconscious mind. But the Word emitted by the Spirit activates the genes deactivated by the transgenerational trauma of sin and restores them to their original reading code, which changes the little percentage of similarity with the animals of Darwin. "All Scripture is God-breathed and is useful for teaching, rebuking, correcting and training in righteousness, so that the servant of God may be thoroughly equipped for every good work" (2 Timothy 3:16–17).

The spiritual person is guided by the Holy Spirit. This can be seen in Jesus, who was coming out of the water of baptism when the Holy Spirit came upon him and drove him into the desert, where he fasted for forty days and was tempted by the devil. So let us not be surprised when we find ourselves in various trials and difficulties. As the apostle Peter says, "Dear friends, do not be surprised at the fiery ordeal that has come on you to test you, as though something strange was happening to you. But rejoice since you participate in the sufferings of Christ, so that you may be overjoyed when his glory is revealed. If you are insulted because of the name of Christ, you are blessed, for the Spirit of glory and God rests on you" (1 Peter 4:12–14).

## Jesus, the Purifying Fire and the Washing-Up Soap

Regarding the coming of Jesus to the earth, the prophet Malachi describes it in the following way:

> "Behold, I send my messenger, who will prepare the way before me; and the Lord whom you seek will suddenly come to his temple, and the angel of the covenant, whom you desire. Behold, he is coming, says the LORD of hosts. And who can bear the time of his coming? Or who can stand when he manifests? Because he is like purifying fire, and like washing-up soap and he will sit down to refine and clean the silver; for he will cleanse the sons of Levi, and he will tune them to gold and silver … So, I will come to put you on trial. I will be quick to testify against sorcerers, adulterers, and perjurers, against those who defraud laborers of their wages, who oppress the widows and the fatherless, and deprive the foreigners among you

of justice, but do not fear me," says the LORD Almighty. (Malachi 3:1–5)

While John the Baptist was baptizing in the Jordan and for the first time presented Jesus, he said, "Behold the Lamb of God who takes away the sins of the world. I baptize with water, but He will baptize you in Holy Spirit and Fire" (Matthew 3:11).

It is the Holy Spirit who guides the actions and thoughts of the spiritual person; on the contrary, what drives the actions of Darwin's human are the biological impulses of the dark unconscious and the instincts. The Holy Spirit is the one who teaches the spiritual person the way he or she should walk. "But when the Spirit of Truth comes, he will guide you into all truth …" (John 16:13).

The most striking example of how the Holy Spirit guides the spiritual person, and not his or her impulses and instincts, we find in the incident when Jesus was baptized in the Jordan River by John the Baptist and from out of the water the Holy Spirit rested upon him in the form of a dove. And then scripture says, "At once, the Spirit sent him out into the wilderness" (Mark 1:12).

Besides guiding him, the Holy Spirit gave him "power":

And Jesus returned in the power of the Spirit to Galilee, and his fame spread throughout the surrounding land. (Luke 4:14)

When he came to the Temple - and the book of the prophet Isaiah was given to him; and having opened the book, he found the place where it was written: "the Spirit of the Lord is upon me …" (Mark 17:18)

# CHAPTER 11

## An Analogy between the Death of Jesus and the Black Hole of Quantum Physics

There is a striking analogy between the plan of salvation of Jesus Christ and the black hole of quantum physics.

A black hole is a place or a region of the universe in which the force of gravity is so strong that no material or particle whatsoever, not even light (and thus his name), can escape from it. It is formed when a star dies.

The scriptures say, "I, Jesus, have sent my angel to give you this testimony for the churches. I am the Root and the Offspring of David, and the bright Morning Star" (Revelation 22:17). And when that Bright Morning Star, Jesus, was dying on the cross, he said, "Father, in your hands I entrust my Spirit," and having said this, like the star that results in a black hole, he expired and died.

Quantum physics says, that the enormous gravitational force that exists there is because of a strong concentration of mass, and it becomes so strong because the latter is compressed into an exceedingly small space, which even light cannot get out of there.

Analogous to that enormous black hole's gravitational force, Jesus took our sins in the cross. 'Surely, he took up our pain and bore our suffering, yet we considered him punished by God, stricken by him, and afflicted. He certainly bore our diseases and suffered our pains; and was considered him scourged, wounded of God, and afflicted. But he was wounded for our transgressions, he was crushed for our sins; the punishment of our peace was upon him, and by his stripes, we were healed" (Isaiah 53:4–5).

When Jesus expired, great darkness came upon the face of the earth: "When it was about the sixth hour, there was darkness over the earth until the ninth hour. And the sun went dark" (Luke 23:44). This is similar to a black hole, which even light cannot escape.

## The Black Hole of Quantum Physics and Death

Experiments show that quantum effects have occurred in the laboratory with nonliving particles. Scientists assumed, of course, that this strange world existed in a world of dead matter and that everything living operated according to the laws of Newton and Descartes, a point of view that has informed all medicine and biology.

The scriptures say the following:

> And he said, "The Son of Man must suffer many things and be rejected by the elders, the chief priests, and the teachers of the law, and he must be killed and on the third day be raised to life." (Luke 9:22)

> Destroy the desires to sin that are in you. Anything that is not clean, a desire for sex sins, and wanting

something someone else has. This is worshiping a god. (Colossians 3:5)

And he gave you life when you were dead in trespasses and sins. (Ephesians 2:1)

Black holes cannot be visualized, although currently, with our technological advances, and especially with our most modern space telescopes, it is possible to locate them.

The scripture says, "But you, Daniel, roll up and seal the words of the scroll until the time of the end. Many will go here and there to increase knowledge" (Daniel 12:4).

A black hole can be exceptionally large or surprisingly small, and there may even be some the size of an atom. The most fascinating thing is that, despite having a size as small as an atom, they can contain a mass equal to that of one of the largest mountains on our planet.

The scripture says, "Because you have so little faith. Truly I tell you, if you have faith as small as a mustard seed, you can say to this mountain, 'Move from here to there,' and it will move. Nothing will be impossible for you" (Matthew 17:20).

The death of Christ is the atonement, the reconciliation of men with God, the granting of a full and free admission back into the precious garden of Eden, from which our ancient disobedient parents were once expelled. But the life of Christ is the Tree of Life in that garden, the source of life, which will work in us the complete transformation of the divine nature. Sin, disease, pain, fear, and death are part of that "transgenerational trauma" that persecutes humanity. Power in our lives—let's fully understand that such power can be achieved only by another higher power. The power of sin and death works throughout our lives. The death of Christ, which is the atonement, reconciles us to God; but only the life of the risen Christ can come against the power of sin and death and free our lives from death and destruction.

When we submit ourselves to our Lord Jesus Christ through the fire of his Spirit, we begin to absorb his energy (the Holy Spirit and fire), and we become that (the black body of quantum physics) until we kill the animal (the genetic inheritance of Adam) in us that is present as a result of the transgenerational trauma of the fear of death and the impulses of the dark unconscious of Darwin's animal, until reaching the measure of the stature of the fullness of Christ (Ephesians 4:13).

## The Catastrophic Curve

A catastrophe occurs when sudden shifts in behavior arise as a result of small changes in circumstances. This may lead to sudden dramatic changes—for example, the black horse of Revelation 6 on the opening of the sealed book. For there to be a swift displacement of "energy-fire" in the horse's colors, it should be a tangerine-colored horse instead of a black horse. This disturbance of a sudden rise of energy-fire leads up to the greenish horse—death.

> Nebuchadnezzar furious with Shadrach, Meshach, and Abednego, and his attitude toward them changed. He ordered the furnace heated seven times hotter than usual, *commanded* some of the strongest soldiers in his army to tie up Shadrach, Meshach, and Abednego and throw them into the blazing furnace. So, these men, wearing their robes, trousers, turbans, and other clothes were bound and thrown into the blazing furnace. The king's command was so urgent and the furnace was so hot that the flames of the fire killed the soldiers who took up Shadrach, Meshach, and Abednego, and these three men, firmly tied, fell into the blazing furnace. (Daniel 3:19:23)

The furnace was so hot that the flames of the fire killed the soldiers who took up Shadrach, Meshach, and Abednego into the furnace, but the three of them did not get burned by the "catastrophic fire." They, the just who serve God, could dwell within the consuming fire; the king's soldiers could not. "'Who of us can dwell with the consuming fire? Who of us can dwell with everlasting burning?' Those who walk righteously and speak what is right, who reject gain from extortion" (Isaiah 33:14,14).

Electromagnetic radiation from heated bodies is not emitted as a continuous flow but is made up of discrete units, or quanta, of energy, the size of which involves a fundamental physical constant (Planck's constant). The heat emitted by the light emitter in Planck's law is analogous to the fire of the Holy Spirit reaching a maximum point, at which it can no longer can be held or contained, leading to death (the catastrophe curve—the death of the old Adam). "But if I say, 'I will not mention his word or speak any more in his name,' his word is in my heart like a fire, a fire shut up in my bones. I am weary of holding it in; indeed, I cannot" (Jeremiah 20:9).

In Wein's displacement curve, with increased heat, color changes from red to orange to green to blue and to ultraviolet in a catastrophic curve. He also observed that as these color waves move from red to orange to green to blue and to ultraviolet, the electromagnetic waves were reduced in size; the more intense the heat, the shorter the curve pattern. In his experiments, Planck also observed that from the green color onward, the thermal heat curve moved differently; its waves became shorter, and it was composed of tiny particles, which he called "quanta," thus beginning the wonderful world of light and color we know as quantum physics.

The green horse of the Book of Revelation is analogous to the green color of the quantum physics experiment explained above. From green radiance on, the behavior of light on a black body is different and cannot be measured with the instruments of Newton's classical physics. The green horse of the Book of

Revelation brings death, similar to the death of the inheritance of the old Adam—fear of death, disobedience, and guilt—to allow resurrection in a "new Adam" according to Christ. "So, it is written: 'The first man Adam became a living being"; the last Adam, a life-giving spirit'" (1 Corinthians 15:45).

The green color in electromagnetic light experiment could be analogous to the green horse of the Book of Revelation bringing death with it—death to the old Adam in you (greenish color, pale horse), and death to the knowledge coming from what you feel, what you see, what you hear, or what someone said but is linked to transcendence beyond what for most people is normal. The same Spirit impels us to move forward to experience the fire of the Spirit in, within, like those 120 in the upper room on the day of Pentecost. It is an intimate personal experience with God, in the loneliness of the desert of trials and temptations (the fire), to make the earthly in us die.

## Nicodemus Syndrome

Nicodemus came to Jesus at night with the external knowledge he had of him in the seminary of life—the things he had heard and the things he had seen in Jesus. "Rabbi, we know that you are a teacher who has come from God. For no one could perform the signs you are doing if God were not with him …" (John 3:2).

Jesus told Nicodemus, "You have to be born again" (John 3:3).

In other words, Nicodemus had to die as "the Morning Shining Star," Jesus, did (in a way analogous to the black hole of quantum physics), and be reborn in a new man (in a way analogous to the white dwarf of quantum physics).

A white dwarf forms when a low-mass star has exhausted all its central nuclear fuel and lost its outer layers as a planetary nebula. After a star dies in a black hole, it becomes a weighty white substance called a white dwarf.

In a vision after his resurrection, John saw Jesus Christ in a way that is analogous to a white dwarf star after a star's extinction: "The hair on his head was white like wool, as white as snow, and his eyes were like blazing fire" (Revelation 1:14).

Dying to the earthly aspect in us is analogous to reaching the point when the believer needs to go beyond his or her beliefs' fundamental doctrines. This means going beyond what one has learned in the seminary, in the church, and in private studies and moving to another spiritual level in a personal experience with the fire of the Holy Spirit with the Risen Christ. It entails no longer living the Christian life according to what we hear from the scriptures or according to others' approval. When we do this, we are no longer guided by the impulses and the instinctive emotional limbic nature, but by the same Spirit that impelled Jesus into the desert, where he fasted for forty days, was tempted by the devil, and began his ministry of salvation in the power of the Spirit. (Colossians 3:5–9).

After Jesus said to his disciples, "After a little while you will see me because I am going to the Father …" (John 16:17), Jesus told his disciples before his trial that he would send the "Holy Spirit who (is with you) and (will be in you)," which would make them reborn for a living hope. They would be "born again" to a spiritual man and woman not vitiated by the works of the flesh, which are of the old Adam inheritance.

At the beginnings of our walks as Christians, our understandings of the ways and the will of our Father were extremely limited. We appropriated the Word of God on a superficial plane and understood spiritual things in naturalistic and external terms: doctrines, traditions, rituals, ceremonies, ordinances, baptisms, communions, programs, blessings, promotions, and activities of the system's old order. Regarding this, Paul tells us, "Therefore, let us move beyond the elementary teachings about Christ and be taken forward to maturity, not laying again the foundation of repentance from acts that lead to death, and of faith in God, instruction about cleansing rites, the laying on of hands, the resurrection of the dead, and eternal judgment. And God permitting, we will do so …" (Hebrews 6:1–3)

When the light of Jesus Christ reflects in humankind (in a way similar to the black body of quantum physics) and as we grow, spiritually speaking, and submit ourselves to the Holy Spirit and fire, and the old Adam dies in us, we analogically become that "black hole," after which the fire of the Holy Spirit of God working on us can be so strong that nothing and no one can escape its attraction, because of the following: "And I, when I am lifted up from the earth, will draw all people to myself" (John 12:32).

# CHAPTER 12

## The Holy Spirit and Fire on the Day of Pentecost

---

While John the Baptist was baptizing in the Jordan, he presented Jesus, saying the following: "I indeed baptize you in water for repentance, but he who comes after me, whose shoes I am not worthy of wearing, is more powerful than I; he will baptize you in Holy Spirit and fire."

Here we observe the double manifestation of how the Word of God is linked, implied, and related epigenetically in the genetic modification of spiritual processes. This is the work that Jesus Christ came to execute in humankind for their restoration and return to the garden from which they were expelled as a result of the first man's transgression of the Creator's supreme law. He, Jesus Christ, who is the image of God, would send his disciples another "Comforter" when he left this world and was no longer physically present with them.

## Another "Comforter–Advocate"

"… The Spirit of truth, whom the world cannot receive, because it does not see him, nor know him; but you know him because **he lives with** you and will be **in you**." (John 14:15–16)

Analogous to natural light, here is the dual function that Jesus, the Word, came to fulfill: "The Comforter," "the Spirit of Truth," had been dwelling with his disciples in the person of Jesus for three years, teaching and consoling them. As the Holy Spirit, he had been for his disciples a teacher, a counselor, a guide, and a friend while he was physical with them, subject to Newton's laws. (They know him because he dwelt *with* them). He had instructed them, had carried their prejudices and ignorance, and had given them comfort in times of discouragement. But he was about to abandon them now. He would give them "another Comforter - Advocate" as compensation for his absence or to perform the functions he would have carried out if he had remained personally with them. And from this we can learn, in part, what the operation of the Holy Spirit is. The Holy Spirit provides all believers with the instruction and consolation that would be given by the personal presence of Jesus being with them. In those moments, Jesus calls himself the Holy Spirit, who was with him for about three years. He was dwelling with his disciples, and his disciples with him.

## The Holy Spirit as Fire

The text continues: "… and will be **in you** - (within you)." By conjugating the verb in the future tense (will be), he referred to his resurrection from the dead on the day of Pentecost, when 120 people received the baptism of the Holy Spirit and fire.

When the day of Pentecost came, they were all together in one place. Suddenly a sound like the blowing of a violent wind came from heaven and filled the whole house where they were sitting. They saw what seemed to be tongues of fire that separated and came to rest on each of them. All of them were filled with the Holy Spirit and began to speak in other tongues as the Spirit enabled them. (Acts 2:1-4)

The "fire" of the Holy Spirit, the tongues, spread like fire over their heads. The thunder of his voice activated the one hundred billion brain cells (neurons) of each of the 120 people there—a large percentage of which remained inactive, owing to the transgression, and 80% of which many scientists call "junk DNA."[38] The external epigenetic factor of the Fire of the Holy Spirit was activated and began to send electrical and bioelectric signals to each other by synapse, the way neurons communicate each other in sending neurotransmission messages.

The abstract spiritual information translated into waves of the cerebral cortex is introduced into the nerve cells, astrocytes, and neurons through their membranes via the receptor proteins. The information that enters with the content of our beliefs, via the nerve cells, is turned into a biological behavioral language—impulses that are sent to the rest of the brain. This will cause changes to occur in how the nerve cells in the brain communicate with each other, and these changes are the foundation that originates our vital brain functions that govern the rest of our biology. Each nerve cell in the brain is impacted by a genome (genes) more diverse than the rest of the cells in the body. This genetic diversity in the brain is what gives neurobiological foundation to the diversity of thoughts. All this is clearly organized by our Creator to give the

---

[38] Dr. Héctor Colón Santiago, "Genetics in the Service of Thoughts," *Christian Neuro Theology*, University of Puerto Rico. It is a course given at the University of "Christian Neuro Theology" of Puerto Rico. Dr. Colón Santiago is a Neuroscientist and Theologian. He is a graduate of the University of Salamanca in Spain.

maximum of physiological specialization in order to sustain the spirit that inhabits the brain. It is because of this foundation that this spirit can relate to the Creator.

Additionally, more than half of that number of glial cells began to communicate through neurosynaptic transmission, too, communicating the message by way of bioelectrical and biochemical discharges to each cell of the neocortex.

Abstract spiritual information with the content of their beliefs was like tongues of fire over the heads of the 120. These were analogous to electromagnetic gamma rays (a strong force of quantum physics), which epigenetically activated the nerve cells and transcribed the message into a natural, behavioral language.[39] (They spoke other languages, which the Spirit gave them to speak).[40] According to divine purpose, these electromagnetic brainwaves synchronized and began to communicate, by synapse, the messages they received from above through the tongues of fire (the gamma rays) and the encoded information of the Holy Spirit..

That abstract spiritual information (ions from outside of their heads) introduced the nerve cells (astrocytes and neurons) through their receptor proteins' membranes. When the content of our beliefs—the information—enters, the nerve cells convert it into language (they spoke in other tongues that the Spirit gave them to speak). And through the neural efferent conduits (neuronal conduits from the cortex to the rest of the physiology),

---

[39] "In the case of the Hebrew alphabet, the 22 graphics used as letters are 22 proper names originally used to designate different states or structures of a single sacred cosmic energy, which is the essence and semblance of all that is. The letters of the ancient alphabets are structured forms of vibrational energy that project forces specific to the geometric structure of creation. In this way, with language you can both create and destroy. The human being enhances the power contained in the alphabets by adding the power of their own intention. This makes us directly responsible for the creational or destructive processes in life. and with just the word!" (Brad Hunter, Creando TuVida, June 18, 2009).

[40] Many of those who witnessed the demonstration believed they were drunk. (See Acts 2:13.)

they convert it into the natural behavioral language of the rest of the organism. Thus was inaugurated that glorious day of Pentecost the "Novus Ordus," the new order—the new covenant between God and men.

Those 120 entered thus the spiritual dimension of communion with the Creator through the Holy Spirit. It activated in them the "seventh sense of spiritual perception ("the executive perception's sense") extinguished and blinded by the mud of sin. The DNA genes that some scientists consider junk began to activate and read the DNA encoded created by the Word in the creation of humankind and turned off by the transgenerational trauma of the fear of death of Adam's inheritance.

This manifestation of the Fire of the Holy Spirit occurred on the day of Pentecost. The Word of God, the Fire of the Holy Spirit, descended with a great roar and strong wind that blew and filled the house where 120 people gathered there waited in an expectant attitude. The strongest and most powerful radiation of the light spectrum (gamma waves [20 to 40 OSC./Seg.]) synchronized in the brain to experience the influence of that spiritual (epigenetic) phenomenon that occurred at those moments. They loudly praised, testified, and boldly expounded the wonders of God as the Spirit gave them to speak.

> Now there were staying in Jerusalem God-fearing Jews from every nation under heaven. When they heard this sound, a crowd came together in bewilderment because each one listened to their language spoken. (Acts 2:5-6)

> "When they heard this sound, a crowd came together in bewilderment because each one heard their language spoken. Utterly amazed, they asked: "Aren't all these who are speaking Galileans? Then how is it that each of us hears

them in our native language? Parthians, Medes, and Elamites; residents of Mesopotamia, Judea and Cappadocia, Pontus and Asia, Phrygia and Pamphylia, Egypt and the parts of Libya near Cyrene; visitors from Rome (both Jews and converts to Judaism); Cretans and Arabs—we hear them declaring the wonders of God in our tongues!" Amazed and perplexed, they asked one another, "What does this mean?" (Acts 2:6–12)

## The thoughts

Spiritual activity, being of a neurophysiological nature, causes the activation of sensations and discharges in the brain that are also subject to perceptions by the individual who experiences them.[41]

Our biology elements are neurotransmitters, cells, hormones, molecules, `amino acids, atoms, DNA, and ions. The distinctive spiritual elements of heaven and that are given by the Creator to us humans in thoughts are intelligence, knowledge, wisdom, truth, revelation, understanding, and purpose. Each time the brain has new spiritual learning, every transcendence in our lives will always cause the brain to make changes in the synaptic connections. That means a spiritual imprint at the level of our neurobiology. -Because the neural connections of our brain are different in

---

[41]  Dr. Hector Colón Santiago, *The Physiology Perspective of Thoughts* (University of Christian Neuro Theology of Puerto Rico). All material from *The Physiology Perspective of Thoughts* is published with permission of Dr. Hector Colón Santiago, president and founder of the University of Christian Neuro Theology of Puerto Rico.

each person who inhabits the planet, it guaranteed the miracle of individuality. All the sophistication and complexity of the brain structures were given to us by the father so that the truths of heaven could be assimilated and understood by those who would seek him in the confines of ages and times.

The brain's inner spiritual feelings can be perceived, interpreted, defined, and obtain meaning from them through thought, like many other experiences where there were emotions, activation of memories, and learning activities.[42]

With this redefinition, we want to categorize the thought process and give it a range of sense of physiological sensory perception and elevate it to its new level of attention, importance, prominence, and transcendence at the level of human affairs. We were significantly elevating ourselves to a new level of understanding, the issues of the Christian faith. The reason that in the neurosciences, there have not been many advances in the study of thought processes is due to the association of thought with the subject of the mind, issues of religions, and philosophical issues, and that have to do with the spectrum of everything that is generated at the level of the brain that cannot be measured scientifically, to that immaterial and abstract entity that gives us the exclusive capacity of our humanity.

---

[42] Dr. Hector Colon Santiago, *The Physiology Perspective of Thoughts*, course #609.

Since God's Word is of an abstract, intangible, and immaterial nature at the level of the brain, we give it meaning, coherence, and sense of transcendence with that physiological activity that is the thoughts. Having the mind of Christ is that we can, like those 120 in the Upper Room, describe, analyze, consider, and give meaning to all the stimuli coming from the inner perceptions activated by the Living Word, which is sharper than the two-edged sword.

Thinking and meditating on the Word becomes a purely molecular biological function, generated by astrocyte cells and neurons through cortical electric waves, strictly abstract and intangible information creating spiritual states of consciousness.

Christians need to know the functions of thought since spirituality is an activity that begins in the plane of abstraction, specifically in the brain. However, it is translated to the rest of our physiology by the mere fact of believing in the Word.

In short, it is through the thoughts that Christians elevate to matters of the spiritual order. They, the thoughts, are the platform of good and evil affairs, of culture's values.[43]

---

[43]   Dr. Hector Colon Santiago, *The Physiology Perspective of Thoughts.*

# CHAPTER 13

## The Holy Spirit and Fire on the Day of Pentecost Is Analogous to Gamma-Ray Bursts and Their Effects on the Human Organism

Health Organizations around the world estimate that about 1 billion people suffer from neurological diseases. "Your whole head is injured, your whole heart afflicted" (Isaiah 1:5).

The human brain, like the entire body, can produce electricity through chemical reactions in its cells. The human body is an overly complex electrical system in which the brain's function is to control and switch. Most of the things we see, hear, smell, taste, and feel result from tiny electrical signals sent from various parts of the body to the brain (bioelectrical signals). "If your enemy is hungry, feed him. If he is thirsty, give him something to drink. In doing this, you will heap burning coals on his head" (Isaiah 55:8–9).

## Optogenetics

Optogenetics is a brain research method that combines optics and genetics to achieve a more rigorous control at a given time, by means of light, of specific events that occur within certain cells of a living tissue.

Neurons work like a solar panel, converting light into electricity. Neurons convert it into bioelectricity to communicate with each other through synapses.

To produce electricity, your body's cell uses a mechanism called the "sodium-potassium gate." When the body needs to send a message from one point to another, the cell opens the floodgate, and sodium and potassium ions can move freely into and out of the cell. Negatively-charged potassium leaves the cell, and positively-charged sodium ions enter the cell. The result is a change in the concentrations of both substances, and it creates electrical charges. This generates a kind of "electric spark."

This spark causes the next cell to do the same, and the next, and so on, like an exceptionally low-voltage electrical storm. And all this because your brain ordered you to move a finger or look at a place, or simply because your heart was readying to give another heartbeat.

Each thought, emotion, or action triggers a reaction in a specific area of your brain. Are you happy? Sad? In love? There goes an electrical storm in your body and your brain! Modern imaging technology allows us to see the intricate dance of energy in the brain, which accompanies every thought and feeling.

The scriptures urge us to always be joyful in the Lord. No matter the alterations in life that may sadden us, there will always be a source of comfort that will make us be at peace and tranquility. "Although the produce of the olive tree is lacking, and the fields do not give maintenance, and the sheep are removed from the fold, and there are no cows in the corrals, yet I will rejoice in the Lord and rejoice in the God of my salvation." (Habakkuk 3:17–18).

In the electroencephalogram of the experiment presented later, in the tracing of the gamma waves in a subject's brain, we observe the activation of these waves. The vibration of the melody of sublime songs of worship to the Creator, accompanied by the musical instruments in perfect harmony, made the peaks of the gamma waves rise to the maximum, as if reflecting the state of spiritual exaltation, before the Divine Majesty, which the subject was in during the experiment.

Electromagnetic fields are used to heat various parts of the body. Heat is generally believed to stimulate natural healing and defense mechanisms to alleviate or cure ailment. The psalmist urges us to praise the Lord because he heals our diseases and all our ailments in a way analogous to the electromagnetic field (Psalm 103:3-5).

Electromagnetic fields are used to work on any psychological problems, from everyday personal or professional issues to traumatic events of different intensities. In the same way, Jesus went throughout Galilee, teaching in their synagogues, proclaiming the good news of the kingdom, and healing every disease and sickness among the people (Matthew 4:23).

Electromagnetic fields help to detect unconscious problems and traumas, especially those unconscious aspects that can sabotage us. The psalmist asks the Lord to guide him in case there is something hidden. (Psalm 139:23-24).

## Quantum Field and Observation

Physicists tell us that when we pass beyond the sphere of subatomic particles, and by extension all that is "real" when we try to look at and understand these particles (quarks, bosons, leptons, and so forth), they are so small that we can't even measure them. There are no instruments available to measure the infinite magnitude of these particles. They are so small that we can only theorize about them. Quantum Physics makes visible the invisible of God's wonderful creation.[44]

By faith, we understand that the universe was formed at God's command so that what is seen was not made out of what was visible. (Hebrews 11:3). Oh, the depth of the riches of the wisdom and knowledge of God! How unsearchable are his judgments, and his paths are beyond tracing out! (Romans 11:33–34).

There is a remarkably interesting fact about these subatomic particles: no one has ever seen them. So if you cannot see these subatomic particles, if you cannot observe them, how can you tell whether they exist? In the scriptures, there is a question analogous to that of the quantum: For who does not love his or her brother and sister, whom has he or she seen? How can one love God, whom one has not seen? (1 John 4:9). It is like a person says: "I serve, and love God, whom he has never seen. But hates his neighbor, whom he sees every day. If you cannot observe God's command, you cannot love Him, either.

We know of the existence of these subatomic particles from the footprints they leave in particle accelerators. In areas where scientists investigate subatomic theories, one can see, even in photography, the footprints these particles leave; and by looking at them, one knows that they have been there. Analogously, Nicodemus came to Jesus at night because he had knowledge of the footprints of Jesus, the visible particle of the invisible light of the True Light, God. "…we know that you are a teacher who has come from God. For no one could perform the signs you are doing if God were not with him" (John 3:2).

There is another interesting aspect of these subatomic particles: they seem to exist only when we observe them. For Elisha to be able to obtain the "double portion" of the spirit of Elijah, he had to observe him in a way analogous to the observation of the quantum subatomic particle. Elijah said to Elisha, "'Tell me, what can I do

---

44  The author, Samuel Padilla Rosa, PhD.

for you before I am taken from you?' 'Let me inherit a double portion of your spirit,' Elisha replied. 'You have asked a difficult thing,' Elijah said, 'yet if you see me when I am taken from you, it will be yours—otherwise, it will not'" (2 Kings 2:9–10).

Both thoughts and feelings have electromagnetic signals. Our thoughts send an electrical signal to the quantum field. Thus, our feelings have the power to "magnetically attract" situations in life.

The scriptures say, "Turn to me and be saved, all you end of the earth; for I am God, and there is no other" (Isaiah 45:22).

## Quantum entanglement

Quantum entanglement is one of the most puzzling phenomena in quantum mechanics. When two particles, such as atoms, photons, or electrons, become entangled, they experience an inexplicable bond that is maintained even if the particles are on opposite sides of the universe. This entanglement is analogous to the scripture text where Jesus said to his disciples that he would not leave them as orphans but would come to them again, though the world would not see him anymore. They would see him, however. Because he lives, they would also live. "I will not leave you as orphans; I will come to you. Before long, the world will not see me anymore, but you will see me. Because I live, you also will live. On that day you will realize that I am in my father, and you are in me, and I am in you." (John 14:18–20).

## Photons of a Protein Entangled

Quantum entanglement also works in biological systems.

Before Jesus's crucifixion, he told his disciples that although the world would not see him anymore, they would see him, because he was going to the Father, and they would be in him and he in them. This would take place on Pentecost with the outpouring of the Holy Spirit and fire, the Advocate in the Upper Room.

> But the Advocate, the Holy Spirit, whom the Father will send in my name, will teach you all things and will remind you of everything I have said to you. (John 14:26)

> But you will receive power when the Holy Spirit comes on you, and you will be my witnesses in Jerusalem, and in all Judea and Samaria, and to the ends of the earth. After he said this, he was taken up before their very eyes, and a cloud hid him from their sight. (Acts 1:8)

> On that day, you will realize that I am in my Father, and you are in me, and I am in you. (John 14:20)

Quantum entanglement implies that any measurement made on the first particle provides information about the result of the measurement on the second particle. Thanks to research, this principle has been proven for the first time in the field of biology. "Philip said, 'Lord, show us the Father, and that will be enough for us. Jesus answered: 'Don't you know me, Philip, even after I have been among you such a long time? Anyone who has seen me has seen the Father. How can you say, "Show us the Father"?'" (John 14:28–29)

## The Thoughts and the Strong Force of the Electromagnetic Radiation of X-Rays and Gamma Rays

Spiritual activity, being neurophysiological, also causes sensations and discharges in the brain subject to perceptions by the individual who experiences them. Since God's Word is abstract, intangible, and immaterial at the brain's level, we give it meaning, coherence, and a sense of transcendence through physiological activity—that is, our thoughts. Having the mind of Christ in us, we can describe, analyze, consider, and make sense of all the stimuli that come from the inner perceptions activated by the living Word, which is sharper than a two-edged sword.[45]

## What If We Had Our Brains 100 Percent Activated?

Currently, the human being uses only 10 percent of his brain, and that tiny percentage reflects our society, which is guided by the transgenerational trauma of Adam's genetic inheritance. That small 10 percent of the brain's capacity is what has humanity in a state of fear, uncertainty, struggles, and wars, behaving like Darwin's animal, guided by the dark unconscious's impulses, and trying to be the strongest to survive and live in the present moment without caring about the future. "Let's eat and drink, we'll die tomorrow" (1 Corinthians 15:32). This seems to be the slogan.

For most people, life is about consistently winning, being the first to arrive. If you do, you will be alone at the top of the tree of evolution, boasting about being superior to the chimpanzee or the orangutan, with a mere one, two, or four percent difference in his DNA sequence.

But what if our brains start to wake up? What would happen to our world if we had 20 percent, 30 percent, or 100 percent of our brains active?

Gamma rays are weightless packets of energy called photons. Unlike alpha and beta particles, which have energy and mass, gamma rays are pure energy. Gamma rays are like visible light

---

[45] Dr. Hector Colon Santiago, *The Physiology Perspective of Thoughts*, 609.

but have much higher energy. Gamma rays are usually emitted together with alpha or beta particles during radioactive decay.

The tongues of fire over the heads of the 120 gathered in the Upper Room on the day of Pentecost is analogous to a burst of gamma radiation—the Holy Spirit and Fire (the Comforter promised by Jesus to his disciples when he was no longer with them). On the day of Pentecost, in the Upper Room, 120 people were invested with the Holy Spirit and fire and began to speak in other tongues as the Spirit enabled them. They received the Holy Spirit and fire, spoke other languages, and, in a way analogous to the most energetic rays in the universe, gamma rays, they received power (Acts 1:1–4).

In the book of Daniel, the prophet prophesies about the day the Lord will reward the people of Israel. They will have plenty to eat, until they are full, and they will praise the name of the Lord, their God, who has worked wonders for them. Never again will the people of Israel be shamed. Then they will know that their Lord is in Israel, that he is their God, and that there is no other. Never again will his people be shamed (Joel 2:25–27). "And afterward, (as in the day of Pentecost in the book of Acts 2), 'I will pour out my Spirit on all people. Your sons and daughters will prophesy, your old men will dream dreams, your young men will see visions" (v. 28).

Before the Pentecost event, the disciples found themselves locked up, filled with fear (the inheritance of Adam's fear) by the events that were taking place with the violence and their Master's death. After that marvelous event of Pentecost, and by the investiture of the Holy Spirit and fire, the disciples were free of that transgenerational trauma of fear that overwhelmed them, to the point that Peter, filled with the power of the Holy Spirit and fire, confronted the same crowd they were afraid of and began to tell them to their faces that they were the same ones who killed him, Jesus, crucifying him by means of wicked men (Acts 2:23–25). "The LORD said to me, 'Son of man, these are the men who are plotting evil and giving wicked advice in this city'" (Ezekiel 11:2).

These wicked people stand in opposition to all Christ represents. "This is the spirit of the Antichrist, which you have heard was coming, and is now already in the world" (1 John 4:3). This spirit, empowered by the evil one and demons, influences religions, governments, education, literature, and entertainment. It is anti-God, anti-Bible, anti-prayer, anti-morality, anti-biblical marriage, and anti-authority. "The coming of the lawless one is according to the working of Satan, with all power, signs, and lying wonders, and with all unrighteous deception among those who perish, because they did not receive the love of the truth, that they might be saved" (2 Thessalonians 2:9–10). But "It is not by might nor by power, but by my Spirit,' says the LORD Almighty" (Zechariah 4:6).

Quantum Physics says ionizing radiation has enough energy to affect the atoms of living cells and consequently damage the genetic material (DNA). But by using that same ionizing radiation energy correctly, cancer cells from DNA can be eradicated. Analogously, the Word of God is alive and active.

> Sharper than any double-edged sword, it penetrates even to dividing soul and spirit, joints, and marrow; it judges the thoughts and attitudes of the heart. (Hebrews 4:12)

> The sinners in Zion are terrified; trembling grips the godless: "Who of us can dwell with the consuming fire? Who of us can dwell with everlasting burning?" (Isaiah 33:14)

These countereffects of ionizing energy happened to King Uzias (2 Chronicles 26:3, 16, 17, 19, 20, 21). Uzziah, king of Judah, was sixteen years old when he became king, and he reigned fifty-two years in Jerusalem. With God's mighty help, Uzziah became very powerful, and his fame spread far. However, as his power increased, Uzziah became arrogant, leading to misfortune. He rebelled against the Lord, the God of his ancestors, and dared to enter the Lord's temple to burn incense on the altar.

Behind him came the high priest Azariah, along with eighty priests of the Lord, all of them mighty men. who confronted him and said, "It is not for Your Majesty to burn incense to the Lord. This is the function of the priests descended from Aaron, since they are the ones who are consecrated to burn the incense. Get out of the sanctuary right now, for you have sinned, and so the Lord God will not honor you."

This angered Uzziah, who was holding a censer, ready to offer incense. But at that very moment, there in the temple of the Lord, by the altar of incense and in front of the priests, his forehead was covered with leprosy. When the high priest Azariah and the other priests saw that Uzziah was leprous, they hurriedly expelled him from there. Moreover, he himself hastened to leave, for the Lord had punished him. King Uzziah remained a leper until the day of his death. He had to live in isolation in his house, and he was forbidden to enter the temple of the Lord.

## Benefits of Gamma Rays

A revolutionary technology known as Gamma Knife is an effective means selectively destroying some types of brain tumors and tackling other abnormalities without the need for incisions in the skull. It is not a scalpel in the conventional sense of the term but an instrument that uses invisible gamma rays. It is practically painless, and its use does not require general anesthesia. It was developed with the cooperation of several of the most notable specialists in radiation teams from all over the United States. With it, a noninvasive treatment is done, without any scarring, disfigurement, or risk of infection. It is a kind of neurological surgery that is performed without damaging adjacent cells.

The Gamma Knife does not cause the patient physical problems, pain, or emotional trauma. It does not require a prolonged recovery, and generally treated patients leave the hospital and resume their normal activities immediately.

## In Agriculture

Gamma rays have the property of breaking the DNA chains of insects and microorganisms, eliminating them or inhibiting their subsequent reproduction. As a result of the processing of food with an adequate dose, pathogenic microorganisms, such as splinter coli, salmonella, and Trichinella spiralis, are reduced by 99.9%. "I will bless the Lord with all my soul; I will bless his holy name with all my being. He is the one who forgives all my evil deeds, who heals all my illnesses" (Psalm 103: 1, 3).

Traces and behavior of Gamma rays can be seen activated in the "Neurophysiologic Verification Experiment of Spiritual Worship" held on July 1, 2017, in Humacao, Puerto Rico. We carried out a brain–mind study in which records and tracings of electroencephalograms were conducted on two of our previously selected partners. The study was conducted while they, like those 120 people gathered in the Upper Room on the day of Pentecost, meditated and worshiped God, "unanimously together" with us. That is, they meditated in the spiritual "invisible" marvelous works of God, which quantum physics makes "visible" with new technologies like the electroencephalogram.

# CHAPTER 14

## Neurophysiologic Verification Experiment of Spiritual Worship

On the first day of July of 2017, in Humacao, Puerto Rico, we carried out a brain–mind study where records and tracings of electroencephalograms were conducted on two subjects (subject 1 and subject 2). These encephalograms were carried out while they, like those 120 people gathered in the High Room on the day of Pentecost, worshiped together with us "unanimously together" to the King of Kings and Lord of Lords.

### Tracing of the Electroencephalogram of Subject 1

The instructions given to subject 1 stated that he was to keep his meditation focused on the sublime things of the Spirit of the living God, the power of the Spirit of God, and prayer.[46] With great expectation, we observed that the activation of alpha waves was constantly reflected in the lines. These waves are usually compatible

---

[46] See appendixes I and II.

with mental states near the border of the conscious with the unconscious. It is in such states where meditation on matters of spiritual transcendence, the process of prayer, and inner relaxation, have ample place. Also, because many areas of the brain are synchronized, states compatible with the feeling of absolute peace are produced. This is indeed in harmony with the type of activity that was done when the participant was worshiping in spirit.

In these waves, a high synchronization of the cerebral cortex is reflected, which translates into an incredibly special cerebral state, because it allows us to continue having a conscious activity at the level of thought—that is, to be fully in control of this activity. Meanwhile, on the other hand, it allows us to access the information that lies in the unconscious state.

In this state, the evocation and perception of multiple memories of a spiritual nature come to light in expectation. This can be translated, according to the scriptures, to when Jesus, the Risen One, instructed his disciples to stay in Jerusalem and wait for the promise that he had given them before he was crucified. "Another Comforter" would teach them all the words he had spoken to them while being "with" them.

He had appeared to the disciples, to whom also, after having suffered, he appeared alive with many indubitable proofs, appearing to them for forty days and speaking to them about the kingdom of God. And while they were together, he commanded them not to leave Jerusalem, but to wait for the promise of the Father, which, he told them, they heard from him. "Because John certainly baptized with water, but you will be baptized with the Holy Spirit within not many days" (Acts 1:5).

## Tracing of the Electroencephalogram of Subject 2

In the tracings of subject 2 the activation of auditory zones was recurrent because of listening to songs of adoration while she, along with us, worshiped.[47] At the beginnings of the songs "Halleluya" and "Your Fidelity Is Great" (plots I and II in appendixes III and IV), in the tracing of "gamma waves," we observed the activation of said waves. The voice vibration of the sublime songs of adoration to the Creator, accompanied by the musical instruments in perfect harmony, is reflected in the strokes of subject 2's encephalogram, which shows constant activation of the brain waves. Chanting and music produced great activity of gamma waves in subject 2's brain, producing a spiritual state of mind linked to the secration of adrenaline and cortisol.

Usually when a person listens to this type of worship or praise music, which is pleasant and meaningful, both the right and left hemispheres tend to synchronize so that the deeper areas of the brain retain these memories, which are easy to consolidate. Genes thus epigenetically marked by the sublime music of worship and praise are activated and read, and they express the information of similar past experiences. Therefore, the experience the person is having becomes a deep memory, as if he were living the experience the first time he lived it.

---

[47] See appendixes III and IV.

# CONCLUSION

Twenty-first century Christians live wonderful moments despite terrorism, misinformation in the media, racial disturbances, atmospheric disturbances, worldwide epidemics, and scientists' disbelief. Many scientific advances in technology—the laser, with its multiple applications; magnetic resonance; transistors; DVDs; fiber optics; tomography; cellular phones; atomic clocks; and GPS—are based on quantum mechanics. The scientific advances of quantum physics have made it possible to reveal and make visible the invisible and marvelous works of God's Creation.

These are the times of which the Lord spoke to the prophet Daniel when he was about to expose the revelation he had given him. "But you, Daniel, roll up and seal the words of the scroll until the time of the end. Many will go here and there to increase knowledge" (Daniel 12:4).

As we saw above, science has made it possible for us to scientifically verify spiritual processes in Christian men and women of the twenty-first century. With the new science of quantum physics, we can see, through high-tech instruments, how the spiritual activity of thinking and meditating on the Word of God causes the activation of sensations and electric and bioelectric discharges in the brain.

Thus we have scientifically evidenced how the Word and music, prayer, and meditation can activate deactivated DNA's genes through the thoughts. That is why we cannot see the spiritual perceptions of the inner brain. As they are light waves, you cannot see them either. They can be perceived, interpreted, and defined, and meaning obtained from them, thanks to science and sophisticated new instruments.

It is through quantum physics that science can study the building blocks of all creation. Now scientists are studying the nuclei of atoms, which contain the most potent energy in the universe. We cannot see the atoms with the naked eye, because they're too small, but scientists have been able to study atoms by using electron microscopes.

One of the most important findings of modern science is the dual (wave–particle) nature of light. With modern instruments of science, scientists found that light has a dual nature. Namely, it behaves both as waves and as particles. Therefore, if natural light, made by the Creator of the universe, behaves in dual form (wave–particle), then God, the True Light, will act as natural light in a dual (spirit–matter) form.

This is the message that we have heard from him and that we announce to you: God is light, and there is no darkness in him. (1 John 1: 5). In the beginning, God said, "Let there be light, and there was light" (Genesis 1: 3).

Everything is made of tiny subatomic bits, but what is the force that holds quantum particles, atoms, and molecules together? The answer is light. From any microscopic algae to the largest planet in the galaxy, everything is made up of matter—elementary particles joined by a kind of glue that makes up the universe and everything that is known.

There are seven primary ranges of wave frequencies within the electromagnetic spectrum of light. Analogously, an angel said to Zechariah that the seven lamps he saw were the eyes of the Lord, which are traveling all over the earth (Zechariah 4:10).

God uses the spectrum of light, from the lowest frequency to the highest frequency, to communicate with humankind. The electromagnetic spectrum includes radio waves, microwaves, infrared rays, visible light, ultraviolet rays, X-rays, and Gamma Rays.

## Radio Waves

The basic building block of radio communications is radio waves. A radio wave is generated by a transmitter and then detected by a receiver. With radio waves, Adam heard the Lord's footsteps in the cool air of the day. They knew that trees obstruct radio waves, and they tried to hide from God. But God used X-rays and gamma rays to penetrate deep through the trees and saw them hiding among the trees of the orchard. Today, if you hear his voice, do not harden your hearts as you did in the rebellion (Hebrews 3:15). There is no created thing hidden from his sight; all things are uncovered and naked before the eyes of the one to whom we must give an account. (Hebrews 4:13).

## Microwaves

With the quantum leap to the higher-energy microwaves, they saw they were naked. (Genesis 3:7). Microwaves can penetrate haze, light rain and snow, clouds, and smoke. Microwaves are used for satellite communication and studying the earth from space. A scatterometer measures changes in the energy of microwave pulses and can determine the speed and direction of wind near the ocean surface. There is an analogy between the teaching of the prophet Jeremiah and the microwave spectrum of electromagnetic radiation. Jeremiah says that the Lord searches the heart and examines the mind to reward each person according to what his or her deeds deserve (Jeremiah 17:10). Mountains and valleys can obstruct or block TV signals. "If your local broadcast tower is behind a mountain or you live in a deep valley, obtaining a good over-the-air TV signal will be problematic, as the signal's line of sight will be blocked or will pass right over your TV antenna.[48]To

---

[48] "Top Sources of Obstruction and Interference That Can Impact Your Over-The-Air TV Reception. https://www.tablotv.com/blog/ota-tv-obstructions-interference-reception/" August 08, 2018

have clear communication with the Lord and a revelation of God's Glory, you have to bring down the mountain of self-pride and selfishness, and lift the valley of depression and pessimism. The rough conduct shall become level, and the rugged places, social misconduct, a plain (Isaiah 40:4, 5).

## Infrared Rays

Like the warmth in the skin produced by infrared rays, two of Jesus's disciples' hearts burned when the Resurrected Jesus opened the scriptures to them. (Luke 24:32). Infrared radiation is that portion of the electromagnetic spectrum that extends from the long-wavelength, or red, end of the visible-light range to the microwave range. Invisible to the eye, it can be detected as a sensation of warmth on the skin. This is analogous to Peter's warmth when denying his Master. It was cold, and the servants and officials stood around a fire they had made to keep warm. Peter also was standing with them, warming himself. (John 18:25).

## Visible Light

Visible light is defined as the wavelengths that are visible to most human eyes. God, the invisible light, makes himself visible in the visible-light portion of the spectrum through his Son, Jesus Christ. God, the True Light, whom no one has seen, was seen in his Son, the Word. The Word became flesh and made his dwelling in us. We have seen his glory, the glory of the one and only Son, who came from the Father, full of grace and truth. The visible light spectrum is the electromagnetic spectrum segment that the human eye can see. More simply, this range of wavelengths is called visible light. We can see the visible light spectrum, that portion of the electromagnetic spectrum that we can see, with the naked eye. God is Spirit, and we cannot see him, but similarly to God's light, we can see him through his Son, the Word who became flesh (Jesus) and made his dwelling among us. We have seen his glory—the glory of the one and only Son, who came from the Father, full of grace and truth (John 1:14). "Philip said, 'Lord, show us the Father and that will be enough for us.' Jesus answered: 'Don't you know me, Philip, even after I have been among you such a long time? Anyone who has seen me has seen the Father. How can you say, "Show us the Father"? Don't you believe that I am in the Father, and that the Father is in me? The words I say to you I do not speak on my own authority. Rather, it is the Father, living in me, who is doing his work.'" (John 14:8–10).

## Ultraviolet Rays

When UVC light shines on water, or if a bulb that emits UVC light is immersed in water, some of the light penetrates the water and is absorbed by germs, such as bacteria and viruses, in the water. When UVC light is absorbed by these germs, they are killed, sterilizing the water. The people of Israel marched through the desert for three days and arrived at Marah, and they could not drink the waters of Marah because they were bitter; that is why they named that place Marah, because its waters were bitter. Then the people murmured against Moses and said, what are we to drink? And Moses cried out to the Lord, and the Lord showed him a tree. He cast it into the waters, and the waters were made sweet. The tree that God presented to Moses is analogous to the effect of ultraviolet rays in the purification of water. The tree represents Christ as the one who purifies our lives and quenches the thirst (John 7:37–38). Ultraviolet light is cost-effective for water purification. "Come, all you who are thirsty, come to the waters; and you who have no money, come, buy and eat! Come, buy wine and milk without money and without cost" (Isaiah 55:1).

## X-Rays

X-rays are electromagnetic radiation that can pass through solid objects, including the body. X-rays penetrate different things more or less efficiently according to their density. In medicine, X-rays are used to create images of the bones and other inner structures in the body. It is analogous to the Word of God, which is sharper than a sword that is double-edged; it penetrates even to dividing the soul and spirit, joints, and marrow. It judges the thoughts and attitudes of the heart (Hebrews 4:12).

## Gamma Rays

A gamma ray is a packet of electromagnetic energy (a photon) emitted by the nucleus of some radionuclides following radioactive decay. Gamma photons are the most energetic photons in the electromagnetic spectrum. In 1967, the OSO-3 satellite made the first significant gamma ray detection from space. This satellite detected a total of 621 cosmic gamma rays. Shortly after, the United States' Vela-5b satellite was originally put into orbit to detect gamma rays originating from nuclear bomb testing. Instead it detected gamma ray bursts from distant galaxies. This was an amazing discovery. It led to a new branch of research related to gamma radiation.[49] Gamma rays have so

---

[49] Safiya Erdogan, "Gamma Rays: Helper or Hazard?" Let's Talk Science, November 23, 2019, https://letstalkscience.ca/educational-resources/stem-in-context/gamma-rays-helper-or-hazard.

much penetrating power that several inches of a dense material like lead, or even a few feet of concrete, may be required to stop them. Gamma rays can pass completely through the human body; as they pass through, they can cause ionizations that damage tissue and DNA. However, gamma rays can also be used to treat cancer. Radiation therapy, or radiotherapy, uses high-energy gamma rays to kill cancer cells and shrink tumors. Gamma Knife radiosurgery is a special form of radiotherapy. It uses beams of gamma rays to treat injured brain tissue by damaging the DNA of dangerous cells. This technique is one of the most accurate and precise radiosurgery systems. It can focus on a small area and avoid damaging surrounding tissues. It can also target cells in the middle of the brain without cutting into the surrounding brain. In fact, only 1 mm of additional tissue around the tumor is destroyed.

In the neurophysiologic verification experiment relating to spiritual worship that was mentioned earlier, the activation of auditory zones in subject 2 was recurrent because of that subject listening to songs of adoration while she, along with the conductors of the experiment, worshiped and meditated on the scriptures. At the beginnings of the songs, "Halleluya" and "Your Fidelity Is Great" (plots I and II in Appendixes III and IV), we observed the activation of gamma waves. The voice vibration of the sublime songs of adoration to the Creator, accompanied by the musical instruments in perfect harmony, is reflected in the strokes of subject 2's encephalogram, which shows constant activation of the brain waves. Chanting and music produced great activity of gamma waves in subject 2's brain, producing a spiritual state of mind, which is linked to the secretion of adrenaline and cortisol, which increase levels of emotional arousal. By increasing the levels of emotional arousal, which involves releasing adrenaline into the body, the amount of attraction between the worshipper and God is also increased.

Oh, the depth of the riches of the wisdom and knowledge of God! How unsearchable his judgments and his paths beyond tracing out! (Romans 11:33)

I pray that out of his glorious riches he may strengthen you with power through his Spirit in your inner being, so that Christ may dwell in your hearts through faith. And I pray that you, being rooted and established in love, may have power, together with all the Lord's holy people, to grasp how wide and long and high and deep is the love of Christ, and to know this love that surpasses knowledge—that you may be filled to the measure of all the fullness of God. (Ephesians 3:16–19)

# APPENDIX I

## Trace 1: Electroencephalogram of Subject 1

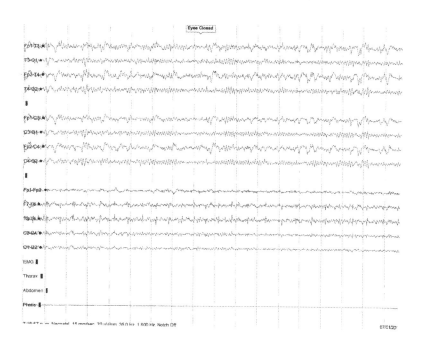

# APPENDIX II

Trace 2: Electroencephalogram of Subject 1

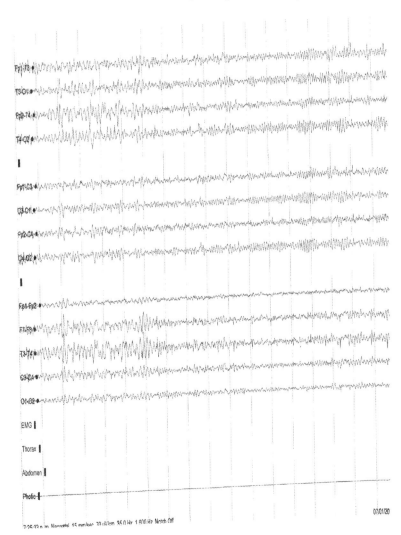

# APPENDIX III

## Trace 1: Subject 2 ("Halleluya" Hymn)

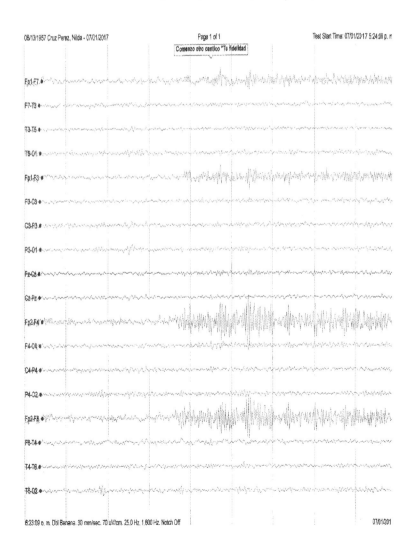

# APPENDIX IV

Trace 2: Subject 2
End of Hymn "Hallelujah,"
Pause, Beginning of Hymn "Tu Fidelidad"

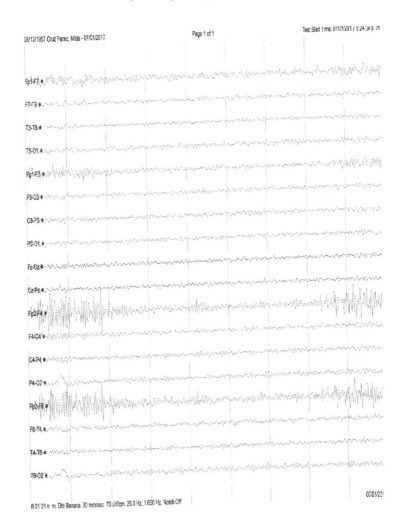

# ABOUT THE AUTHOR

 After returning from the Vietnam War (1966-1967), and waging another war with himself, due to the traumas resulting from the experiences suffered on the battlefield, Samuel Padilla Rosa obtained an associate degree on Social Studies, from the Puerto Rico Junior College. He also acquires a bachelor's degree in economics, with classes in psychology and comparative literature, from the University of Puerto Rico. Before dedicating himself to the ministry of the church and obtaining a master's degree in theological studies, he worked as an economist for the Government of Puerto Rico and as a teacher in the Public Instruction System. In 2005 he moved to the New York City. While he was serving as co-pastor at Elim House of Worship in Lower Manhattan, along with Senior Pastor Carlos Torres Oyola, he co-founded a youth rehabilitation center in Newark, New Jersey. After returning to Puerto Rico, he obtains a Ph.D. in the incipient branch of neuroscience – Christian Neuro Theology – he is the author of more than a dozen books. Currently Dr. Samuel Padilla Rosa is committed to teaching and preaching the gospel of Jesus Christ.

Printed in the United States
by Baker & Taylor Publisher Services